Dear All

Dear All,

A collection of Round Robins

ANDREW DUFFY
CAROLINE DUFFY
OLIVER PUGH

Icon Books

Published in the UK in 2004
by Icon Books Ltd, The Old Dairy,
Brook Road, Thriplow, Cambridge SG8 7RG
email: info@iconbooks.co.uk
www.iconbooks.co.uk

Sold in the UK, Europe, South Africa
and Asia by Faber and Faber Ltd,
3 Queen Square, London WC1N 3AU,
or their agents

Distributed in the UK, Europe, South Africa
and Asia by TBS Ltd, Frating Distribution Centre,
Colchester Road, Frating Green, Colchester CO7 7DW

Published in Australia in 2004
by Allen & Unwin Pty Ltd,
PO Box 8500, 83 Alexander Street,
Crows Nest, NSW 2065

Distributed in Canada by
Penguin Books Canada,
10 Alcorn Avenue, Suite 300,
Toronto, Ontario M4V 3B2

ISBN 1 84046 631 6

Design by Phillip Appleton

Printed and bound in the UK by Clays, Bungay

CONTENTS

DEDICATION

Andrew and Caroline: To friends and family – 'All the world is strange, exceptin' thee and me. And even thee's a little strange…'

Oliver: To Emily and Stanley.

ACKNOWLEDGEMENTS

Andrew and Caroline: We would like to thank all those people who have shared their lives and their stories with us, fuelling our imaginations and our book. And heartfelt thanks to those who have put up with our own Round Robins – especially those who were honest.

Oliver: I'd like to thank Amy for her rather nice handwriting on the cover, The Brewster for designing me a couple of fancy crests while simultaneously trying to teach me about colour, and last but by no means least, Phillip, for putting everything, including me, in its place.

FOREWORD

Round Robins – the Christmas-card enclosures we love to hate, but read with relish. We laugh, we groan, we shake our heads at how remarkably dull Aunt Edie's life is, how tediously self-satisfied those former neighbours have become, how suspiciously perfect Jim and Anita's children have turned out to be.

Some of us even send Round Robins, 'against our better judgment', because 'they do help to keep in touch'. Naturally, our own missives are a wry, tongue-in-cheek, post-modernist, self-aware, witty-but-wise take on a life well lived. We project ourselves, and what we want our lives to be.

Happy delusion! The dark secret of the Round Robin is that it reveals more about us than we ever wanted to show. Even the safest one tears down the thin veil that defends our fragile psyches against the harsh glare of a hostile world. Or, in this case, our family and friends.

'Oh wud some pow'r the giftie gie us/Tae see ourselves as others see us', wrote Robbie Burns. He thought he was being perceptive. In fact, he was just revealing the mire of self-doubt and secret inadequacy that tormented him in the wee small hours when he was woken by the crushing memory of the childhood event that prevented him from ever living a happy, fulfilled adult life. Probably. We don't know for sure. He never wrote to us at Christmas.

Christmas is a time of celebration, so here is a celebration of the human condition, comic, tragic or both, seen through the festive prism of the Round Robin. Let us not forget, the next time we summarise our own year into a single side of folded A4, that it says so much more about us than we ever wanted to say. And at the same time, may we never take ourselves too seriously.

Andrew and Caroline Duffy (Christmas 2004)

All characters in this book are fictitious, and any similarity to persons living or dead is entirely to be expected.

THE ANNOYING HIGH ACHIEVERS

Jinty, Jeff, Jemima, Julian and Jessica Phillips excel at whatever they do, without trying too hard. They are blessed with beauty, brains, talent and drive.

Their children have never had a pimple or single day's self-doubt.

They live in a modest family house in the Home Counties; they could afford bigger, but they give a lot of their money to people less fortunate than them, which is pretty much everyone.

They send their Round Robin to all their friends and family.

Some use it to encourage their own kids to excel like the Phillips children.

Others just laugh hollowly and throw it away.

The Willows,
Silver Lane,
Amersham,
Bucks HP2 1AP

Dear All,

Time again for the annual catch-up with the Phillipses. And there's a lot of catching up, as we've all been super-busy!

Jemima (15) is studying hard for her O-levels, and her teachers say they will be disappointed if she doesn't get all As, to add to the four she got last year. She's growing up into such a lovely tall girl, with long blonde hair. The Storm scout said that's what caught his eye, and Jem's just done Julian Macdonald's Paris show, Givenchy in Milan and Vivienne Westwood in London. She flies first-class everywhere, and good old Rocinante, our Volvo, is having a hard time keeping up with her as we race around Europe from catwalk to catwalk. She's just had a range of dolls launched, based on her, called Jem'z Frenz, which will be in the shops for Christmas. Sadly, Jem's been so busy, she's had to turn down the album with Britney and Christina, but she says there's only so much a girl can do!

Julian (11) is still as football mad as ever. His highlights of the last year were scoring the winning goal in the European Under-18 League and being invited to try out for Leeds. He's not sure – even though Auntie Jill lives nearby in Bradford – because he's also had offers from Bayern Munich and Real Madrid. He also still plays chess when he has the time, and he spent a very cheerful week in May in Moscow training other Grand Masters. He says it keeps his mind sharp, which helped him when Microsoft asked him to patch up the problem with the Trojobot virus. His other good news is that he passed the 11-plus and has a place at the grammar school.

Jessica (10) came top in her class in French, Maths, Science, History and Social Studies, and won the school prize for Domestic Science, which didn't really surprise us, after the success of her series, Pressure Cooker Kids, on Channel 5. She also started ballet lessons last year, and she's come on in leaps and bounds (!). She made her debut at Covent Garden with Sylvie Guillem in July. The Telegraph described her performance as "A dazzling display of naïve brilliance and rare dramatic grace, well supported by Ms Guillem." Now Jessica has just finished choreographing the new Bono/Eno Swan Lake-Redux, and she'll be touring with Sylvie to New York, Berlin, Paris, Vienna, Beijing and Tokyo in the spring. Look out for postcards!

Jeff (40 this year!) remains committed to halving Third World debt by 2010, and ensuring a clean water supply to sub-Saharan Africa by July. He's travelling a lot, which gives him time to write, and the third volume of his biography of Edwina Currie (the other woman in his life!) has just gone for final proofing. The Rolling Stones have asked him to tour with them again in August and he's told Mick he'll let them know. It clashes with our usual Kathmandu-to-Kilimanjaro overland, which the kids love so much. This year we want to spend a week en-route working with Cambodian dump children and reintroducing democracy into Myanmar, so I've told Jeff that Mick and Keith may just have to postpone the tour.

And me (no age given!)? I'm still – just – keeping it all together.

We haven't sent Christmas presents this year, but instead have donated to charity. I urge everyone to do so too.
Special Christmas love to you all,
Jinty, Jeff, Jemima, Julian and Jessica

THE RETIRED MAJOR-GENERAL

Maj-Gen Godfrey Talbot's brother Marcus inherited the country house, the title and the seat in the Lords. What was there left for Godfrey to do, but join the Army?

Godfrey was always second fiddle to Marcus, and even in retirement, is still in his shadow.

Other soldiers spend a career in the army being soldiers: Godfrey spent his social climbing and making connections with some of the right people.

His Round Robins are sent to absolutely everyone, and aim to impress and namedrop. But unfortunately, few people have heard of the many names he drops.

He was secretly disappointed not to get a knighthood, and his wife, Vanessa, also rather wanted to be Lady Talbot.

Godfrey still scans the Birthday Honours list, just in case.

Hepton Manor
Nr Hepton Magna
Salisbury
Wiltshire

Dear All,

With the season of mists and mellow fruitfulness truly past and done with our thoughts turn as ever to friends near and far. Our thanks as ever to those whose hospitality has meant so much to us over the last twelvemonth. In January we stayed with our great friends Sir Toby and Lady Millicent Grippe-Fanshawe (he was Ambassador to Liechtenstein at the end of the Cold War, she did that portrait of the Duke of Northumberland that Brian Sewell was so horrid about) in Washington. He still has the ear of the senior George Bush, and discreetly gave me the nod that we'll be out of Iraq by Christmas. Just as well – Toby and Millie's boy Oliver has some gilt-edged deals in Saudi, so it wouldn't do to rock the boat.

February, as ever, found us in sunnier climes when our dear friend Sheikh Akhbadi invited us to Dubai. Unfortunately we just missed the races, as there were no Air Miles seats on the right dates. Put the Sheikh in touch with my old chum Major Rupert Hetherington (who was just back from another close attempt on the South Pole), which one hopes will bear fruit before too many suns have risen and set. Mum's the word, but I think we'll all be happier with the way Mr Ghadaffi behaves over the next months.

We spent April in Verbier, as ever was, staying with our great friends Gerald and Gillian Massingberd (his grandfather was briefly Viceroy at Omdurman, her mother was the chocolate heiress who caused that hoo-hah just after the Coronation). It was getting towards the end of the season so the snow wasn't its best, but Gerald and Gillian's warm hospitality more than made up for it, before they themselves had to leave for Rome. Besides, since the crash on the Cresta in '77, I haven't been as spry on my skis as I'd like.

In July we stayed at our great chums the Stanhope-Fry's charming cottage in the grounds of Chartwell (Hugo just missed the Earldom when that Canadian cousin turned up and married the second wife's third daughter, Deirdre I think her name was, with the hare lip and the gammy leg) while they were at their place in the Dordogne. Had a dreadful episode with the burglar alarm, and the boys in blue weren't at all polite. Vanessa has never felt comfortable with the police since our dear friend Sir Charles Rifkind had to resign as Commissioner over that sad episode with the call girl, Daphne I think her name was, and that odious chap from the Mirror, or was it the Mail, my memory isn't what it used to be.

September saw the christening of our fifth granddaughter (Jonnie married that Catholic girl, Maddie, whose father was so nearly archbishop of Pontypridd) and a chance to stay in Cornwall with our dear old friends Julian and Phang-Mai Petherbridge-Wetterington (Julian was our man in Burma for more years than he cares to recount, she's that Vietnamese girl he married after poor old Olivia had that ghastly episode with the Moulinex). They've just had to close the safari park after some run-in with some dreadful little animal-rights activists, who let the tigers out. Had to call in Toby's boy Oliver (who trained with the SAS at Hereford) and a few of his City chums before the police got wind of it, and I think we can rest assured that the residents of Bodmin can sleep more soundly in their beds now.

November 25 was the regimental reunion, this year at the In and Out, sadly without the presence of the dear Prince of Wales, who had a prior engagement with some lights on Regent Street. Instead, our dear friend Brigadier Geoffrey Temple-Prosser gave a sterling speech, some of which sadly didn't quite reach us at the back of the mess hall. Still, the Tans and Blues thrives, and that's enough to carry one into the New Year with fortitude and vigour.

Hope this finds you as it leaves us, filled with the Christmas Spirit.

Yours aye,

Godfrey + Vanessa

THE WALKING DISASTER

Bad things keep happening to Jill Carter – but at least it gives her something to talk about.

Her life has always been defined by suffering: she spent her youth caring for her parents as they dwindled away through a series of quiet illnesses.

Now Jill is 49 and alone, and lives in a twee terraced cottage with a neat garden.

She's not ambitious, and has never really given herself up to the idea of work. She lives a quiet life, and enjoys gardening, reading and recuperating.

She sends her Round Robins to old family friends and work colleagues, and the nurses who know her so well.

Ward 7
Westchester County Hospital
Kingston upon Hull

Dear All

After such a trickey year last its been nice to take things more easy this. Not that its been as quiet as Id like, Id only just settled the court case over last years bump in Morrisons carpark where that pharmacist reversed into my bicicle sending me flying and chipping my cocyx which still gives me twinge's. The magistrate was very understanding and the settlement was a goodly sum, but I have'nt really found it as easy to get about as I used and sometimes if I stand up quick I get a shooting pain down the rib's on my left, and my shouder throb's a bit.

I had another accident at Greenfingers our local garden center where my trolley had one of those wobbley wheel's which makes it go all not straiht besides my shouder was hurting a lot and anyway the trolly hit into a shelf of begonnia's which fell down and knocked a gnome on to my foot. It was funny seeing him sitting there with a cheekey grin but it did hurt a lot and the doctor said Id bruise'd my angle and put it in a plaster. I coud'nt drive for three week's and the office was very sympathtic and Phyllida from bought ledger came round with some files so I could do my work from home it was nice of you many of you to visit me, and Greenfingers gave me the tray of begonnia's as part of the settlement which also paid for a nice conservatory out the back and a 2nd-hand Renaut megane in green which is nice because its high so I can see the road a lot.

June saw me back at work, but then in the summer sale's at John Lewis' an elderly lady drove into the back of me on the slip-road she said she had not had more than one sherry but I got whiplash and my Renaut was a right off. The old ladys insurer's settled out of court, well she was in her 80s and she didn't have much of a case so it was all cleared up niceley and put another tidey sum in the bank although it does'nt help when the damp weather comes in and my necks so stiff I cant hardly turn it. The office was sympathtic and said I could extend my sick-leave indefinateley as Phyllida was already doing a lot of my job so its an ill wind like they say.

The damp spell over the autum was a bit trickey though and my reumhatism likewise my lunbago was flaring up so I spent a bit of the settlement from Morrisons bump on a month walking in the Alps although with my angle still being sore from the gnome I had to take it slow and steady especially on the hills. I had a nasty slip on the Matterhorn and bruise'd my hip quite badley, but the Swiss goverment was very sympathtic and agreed with my lawyer that the mountian was steeper than there was any real need for and there were'nt adequate signage warning people how slippey the ice got and their settlement was very generous, well their Swiss are'nt they? What with one thing and another I don't have to work as much as I used and what with Phyllida doing my job I told the office I was going to leave.

Ill be spending Xmas at the Westchester again because theres something wrong with my stomoch and the doctor's cant seem to find out what it is so their keeping me in for test's but their very friendley and the nurse's are taking good care of me and haveing them on call 24hrs is a blessing. But its not been a bad year all things considered and now next year if my twinge's and ache's allow me Ive been thinking that it would be good for me to do a counseling course because after all Ive been through I can be very sympathtic to other peoples trouble's and a lot of my life experience's can be valuable to them.

Take care of yourselve's this festive season.
Love,
Gill.

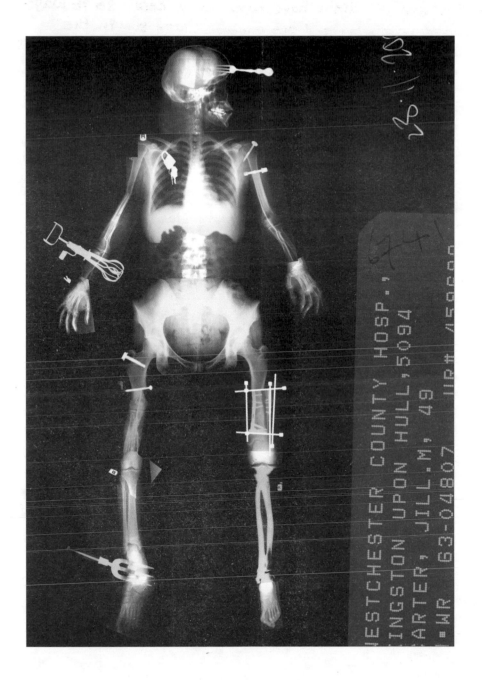

THE DOWNSHIFTERS

Emily and Stephen Norrington are living the dream. The money they made on their Victorian terraced house in Chiswick has allowed them to buy a farmhouse in Somerset near the M5 (it's Georgian, but noisy when the wind's from the south).

Stephen is working in a gentle law practice in Yeovil. The big house, garden and children occupy Emily. The children, Sophie and Oscar, have taken to it like ducks to a village pond.

They write their Round Robin to London friends who have yet to make the move – and have no intention of doing so.

As yet, Somerset hasn't embraced these out-of-towners, and won't do for a few more generations.

Stephen makes every excuse to get back to London, and Emily is secretly already wondering if she really preferred Chiswick.

It's very dark at night, and they can hear the noise of the cars driving past their house to cities where there are restaurants, theatres, shops and life.

Manse Farm, Lane End, Coddington, Somerset

Dear All,

Well, we've finally done it! This spring we made the move from London W4 and are now the proud owners of Manse Farm, a gorgeous 18th-century farmhouse near Coddington. Green views and timeless Englishness wherever you look. It's all very Thomas Hardy. Instead of the District Line, Stephen drives along country lanes to his new job at Trubshawe Jeffries and Partners in Yeovil. He says the law moves more slowly in the country. He's also become an avid fan of Radio 4. I often see him sitting in the car chortling to I'm Sorry I Haven't a Clue. It's something I try to discourage as he knows 7pm is the "the witching hour", bath time for the twins. We are mooting another car when finances are more settled. Sometimes I dream of the old days when I had to wait 15 minutes for the bus to Charing Cross. Here, there's one bus into Yeovil on Tuesday for market day, and one back on Thursday. Like I said, <u>very</u> Thomas Hardy.

We have lots of plans for refurbishing the barn, as soon as Stephen is made a partner which he tells me cannot be more than three years away, with his City experience. It's just a question of waiting for one of the partners to retire… or die. In the meantime, I've enjoyed planting a vegetable garden on one corner of our rolling acres (all three of them!). Unfortunately, Stephen's goat, Buster, ate our first crop so at weekends he likes to drive back to Trouts 'n' Sprouts in Islington. It's awfully expensive, but he says they do the best fresh vegetables in the country. I'm sure the local farm shop is adequate, but he insists.

The twins have settled well at the primary, and don't seem to miss the terra firma of Chiswick pavements. They love the mud, especially traipsing it through the house. Their walk to school is ten minutes across a field on a track that seems to get muddier each time they walk across it. We are now the proud owners of 15 pairs of wellies. My soft leather Russell and Bromleys have been relegated to the old apple store along with an awful lot of my wardrobe. I'm still wondering if mud-stained jeans and Barbour are really <u>me</u>.

The Gap Kids' card has been replaced with a Homebase card and a damp-proof course for the kitchen. We bought a wonderful refurbished Aga from Iron John in South Kensington, but we're having trouble getting it installed. It seems Coddington builders are as unreliable as those we left behind in London.

We've built the twins a tree house in the orchard, but Buster ate the rope ladder, and Stephen had to go to London to get an aluminium one from Peter Jones. I miss friends in London, although we seem to have had an endless stream of visitors down for weekends, which has kept us busy. Sometimes we feel a bit like we are running a B&B! Perhaps if we charged we could afford that second car...

When we were not hosting London friends here I've managed a couple of trips up to the Big Smog myself. Good to catch up of some retail therapy, museums and restaurants. Charity raffles in the village hall don't have the same appeal and going to the village shop for a pint of milk and postage stamps does not satisfy those Kings Road twinges.

Still, the local pub is good, Stephen tells me, and he has started playing cribbage. I'm signing up for an organic gardening course in Feb. Then there's the Easter parade, the village fete in July, Bonfire Night and something called Grindling in November, which seems to involve the children visiting newcomers to the village and demanding money with menaces. They've been doing it in Coddington since 1420, apparently. And so the country year rolls on!
Do hope to see a few more of you down in the New Year.

With all our love this Festive Season,

Emily, Stephen, Sophie and Oscar (and Buster!)

THE INNOCENT NUN

Praise be for Sister Agatha Mary!

She became a nun at 21, and spent the first twenty years in a closed order.

Now she has joined an open community in the West Country, and is involved in outreach programmes with the wider world.

Blissful in her innocence, many of the challenges of modern living pass far over Sister Agatha Mary's head, leaving her faintly bemused, but always smiling.

She sends her Round Robins to her family, and all the convent associates on her prayer list.

She is warm, twinkly, and getting increasingly broad in the beam thanks to her religious devotion to cake.

✝ he Convent of the Holy Sisters of the Annunciation,
The Old Rectory,
Piddletrenthide,
Somerset

Dear All

My dears, I do so hope this letter finds you all well and able to reflect on a year fruitfully lived. This year we have welcomed two new novices, which is always exciting. One has left behind her life as a professional wrestler, while one was a new convert from our outreach to prostitutes in London. I'm sure with their wealth of experience they will be instructive additions to our close-knit little sisterhood.

I have been made Sister in charge of the Kitchens this year so have learnt a lot from that delightful young Jamie Oliver off the television and enjoy creating things with the bumper crop we've been blessed with from our vegetable garden, as well as making some rather wicked cakes. Have you ever tried butter icing with sherry? I do like to follow the Celtic tradition of praying in all circumstances of our daily lives and I certainly find lots of sources for prayer at the oven. The other Sisters say I am a liability, and at the table our daily bread, or in our case cake, is always something to give thanks for. Sister Wendy is doing a sterling job loosening our habits!

After my six-week silent Ignation retreat at Easter, I had the opportunity to take a most enjoyable summer vacation this year. Our dear associate, Guy Rogers, such a nice young man, let me house-sit his home in Docklands. Guy's apartment had lovely views across the City and was very artistically decorated with simply immense black-and-white photographs of handsome - if a little naked for my tastes - young men by someone called Helmut Newton. One of the many young men who share the converted warehouse, who I believe is a fashion designer, tells me Guy's style is minimalist and art haus, whatever that means.

The neighbourhood had a nice community feel, but it was strange to see so many good looking young men, but so few young ladies. I'm no expert in the ways of the world, but I would have thought the girls of London would be flocking there. My blue habit must have been a strange sight in that trendy quarter. Perhaps they could not believe I was a real nun.

London was such a refreshing change from the rural peace of the convent. I really enjoyed the buzz of Central London and managed to visit a few galleries. I managed to catch up with the latest Lloyd-Webber and a very refreshing play at the Royal Court about shopping, which again I confess had rather more nakedness in it than I am used to. But Adam and Eve were naked, so I must keep an open mind. I also had time to finish my tapestry of the Annunciation for the Lady Chapel, and spent evenings carrying succour (and cake!) to the homeless. I was delighted to find an Indian cake shop in Brick Lane, were there were some particularly delicious ones made with pistachio and condensed milk. Mmm, God is good! I keep meaning to try that here, but we do not grow many pistachios in the garden so I will have to try with hazelnuts.

I am still doing my three mornings at the special school in Taunton and so enjoy the drama classes. My students and I put on a little show at the local community centre depicting the lifecycle of the butterfly, using music, dance and colourful costumes made from egg boxes. We got rave reviews in the Taunton Herald, and the students were so chuffed, the dears, after I had read it to them and explained what it all meant.

Better dash, as I want to bake our four-foot butterscotch and whiskey Christmas cake for the advent meditation.

May the spirit of the Lord bless you all this Christmas.

In His name

Sister Agatha Mary

Sister Agatha Mary

THE TEEN BLOGGER

Alicia Redfern, thirteen, writes all her innermost thoughts in her online diary – My So-Called Blog – for anyone browsing the Internet to read. She doesn't use her real name, of course.

Most of Alicia's innermost thoughts are about herself, her boyfriends, herself, her best friends, herself, her ex-best friends, herself and herself. In that order.

She writes her blog to share her thoughts with the world, because they are really quite deep, and because everyone else in her school is doing it.

Luckily for her, she has no idea that most of her readers are middle-aged men.

If she did, she'd think that was gross.

Ewwww.

December 12th

I have the MoST BOrInG life EVER! I need to do something really STrANgE, like kiss my best friend (Ewwww!!!). Today is also the WoRsT day of my life, all because of J. It sucked. I rEaLLY want a boyfriend but I don't know if it should be J, because I think J only wants to have a girlfriend just so he has one. He's so IMmAtURe, even if he is a bit of a cutie!! (how many 14-year-old boys have six-packs?)! Boys are funny. I got my first boyfriend, P, at the beginning of the year, but he was completely USeLeSS. I MeAn, SEriOUSly! I'm not even sure if he liked me. He never talked to me or anything. Or went anywhere with me. Or looked at me. Or knew who I was. So I asked my friend to tell him I didn't want to be his girlfriend anymore, and she told me he just shrugged and said "WhaTEvER!!!!" What is it with boys????

Every day I change. Sometimes I can see it, and it's really interesting. I hope I turn out to be the kind of person people can give the gift of LoVE to. Because I think the gift of LOvE is the biggest gift in the whole world, really. It was like on Xena, Warrior Princess, when she gave Lord Orku the gift of life and he repaid her with his love, even though she couldn't take it because he was King of the Dead or something. That was SO SweET!!! I wish someone would do that to me.

I haven't been lucky with boys ever since D. I had this BigGEsT CruSH on D for months. There was this school disco and at the end me and my friends did this dare where we had to kiss the boy we were dancing with, and I was with D. But then my dad walked in just when I kissed him (D, guys, not my dad - that would be too ewwwww!). Dad was angry, but D was really into it. He even asked me over to his house when his Mum and Dad were out and he put on this scary film I think it was so he had an excuse to sit next to me. But then he kissed me during one of the gross parts where this alien exploded and there was all slime everywhere so I closed my eyes, and he asked me if he was doing it wrong which is SOOO UncOOL! Sometimes I wish I was someone else, who didn't have all these ProBLeMS and PrESSurES!!

Just cHiLLiNG now. Got Avril on the i-pod, some live trax I ripped off a cool site. Man, she knows what it's about!!!!

I've gone through six boys this year, and I think I'm turning into a MaN-EatER. I have to be nice to boys tho, because it's Christmas soon and I want to get lots of cards so everyone will see that I am POpuLAr, really. Not like my ex-Best Girl Friend, who sent all those cards to herself last year which was rEaLLY UNcoOL, even if I did send some of them but that was only because she asked me to.

It's raining now. I love rain. It's like the tears of heaven WeePiNG for the sadness in the world, but rain brings new life to the world, too, with flowers and stuff, except not in December. Then it just makes things wet. Sometimes I think I must be an especially sensitive person to think things like that, because whenever I tell my friends about them they look at me like I'm STrAnGE. But I know that it's me, deep inside.

I suppose that's why sometimes I just want to be AlonE. But now I'm going to this party with this boy, J, who I've always liked a lot but he ignored me until last week when for no reason he smiled at me and said "Hi!" so he must really like me a lot. At least I hope he does!!!! Sometimes, I really like being me!!! I'll write more tomorrow!!!!

31

THE INDIAN COMPUTER WHIZ

Pradeep Rajapalakrishnan is 28, elegantly tall, with the rakish good looks and groomed moustache of a Bollywood heart-throb.

He's also something of a whiz with computers.

He's the oldest son, and the pride of his extended family in Chennai. His mother has been looking for a suitable wife for a long time, but no one is ever quite good enough for her Pradeep.

He has broken her heart by leaving India to work in England.

Luckily he has an uncle who can keep an eye on him.

She needn't worry. Pradeep is a good boy, and not one to be tempted by the fleshpots of the West.

He's also hard-working, ambitious, and one day soon he will make his family proud of him.

He writes his Round Robin for his mother, his father, his brothers and sisters, and all his dozens of aunties, uncles and cousins.

A Sound Vision Ltd
Crick-Watson House,
Newton Technopreneur Zone,
Leeds
West Yorkshire LL8 3NA

Dear All,

Whilst everything in Great Britain closes down for
Christmas, it is so very peaceful that Mumbai
seems to be a great distance away! Cousin Ravi
and I have been nose to grindstone here, and as
a result we are sorry that we cannot come home
to spend the festivity with dear family and
friends.

I recall how when we left at the start of year,
many people said that we were crazy to work in
IT in Yorkshire when it is booming so in
Bangalore. It is true that we both did indeed
find it hard at first, but Uncle Govindan and
Auntie Vela have been so very kind as to let us
sleep in their front parlour, and we could save
up money. Our workmates were not so welcoming,
though, and there were often jokes about
poppadums and something called chicken tikka
masala, which was new to our ears. They seemed
to think that we are here to take their jobs, and
many people would call us Paki, which made Ravi
and I laugh so much at their ignorance! Uncle
Govindan explained to me that it is because of
their shameful lack of geographical fundamentals
and systemic weaknesses in their education
programmes that have crumbled so much since
Grandfather's day.

But Ravi and I have tried hard to make something
of ourselves and by dint of working 16 hours
every day, our fortunes have improved. I know
some of my dear friends and family are not up to
top-speed with tech-speak, so I will hope to
enlighten you. Sound/Vision is a new vocal-
transformation programme Ravi and I have been
working on which will disguise the Indian accent
as British. This means there will be no need for
voice training at call centres, with a resulting
reduction in training costs. With S/V, an Indian

team can be call-centre ready at the drop of a
hat. The S/V programme requires pattern-
recognition from all kinds of British accent, and
it was thus that we came here to the motherlode
of the language.

Our good fortunes picked up after July (in which
month we were sorry to miss India's sterling
performance at Headingley!), when we signed deals
with IBM, Phillips, the National Westminster
Bank, and Reuters, and we have set wheels in
motion for an IPO next summer. Ravi has just
flown to Seattle to catch-up with the old friends
from our Harvard days who want a piece of the
S/V action. I miss him and my family. The good
news is that I have just bought a splendid house,
with 12 bedrooms and a very fine Corinthian-styled
stone portico, just the stone's throw from
Headingley. It was being sold by a footballer who
was obligated to pay the sky-high legal expenses
after a shocker of a court case. At only 3
million pounds, it compares very favourably with
current property values in Mumbai. It also has a
fine gravel drive and a good-sized garage, which I
will need as I have ordered spanking new Aston-
Martin DB9, which I know that Uncle Pani will
enjoy driving when you all come to stay. But now
that we are the proud bosses of 200 employees at
A Sound Vision, as well as making time to go to
the temple each day to pray to Ganesha, I don't
drive as very often as I would like!

I am meeting more Indian people here, which is
lifting my spirits somewhat. Last weekend Mr
Jerry Hinduja invited me to put a million pounds
stake in the next Aishwarya Rai hit film, which
means I can get her autograph for Cousin Nirmala.
And yesterday I received a Christmas greetings
card from Mr Tony Blair and his family, inviting
me to pass a weekend at Chequers with them in
May. I hope many of you will be able to join me
in Great Britain for that!

With warm salutations to all my dear family and
friends for this holiday season,

Pradeep

THE UNMARRIED AID WORKER

Claire White became an aid worker in her idealistic early 20s, after reading Cultural Studies at the University of East Anglia.

Nearly fifteen years later, with a failed engagement behind her, she's a fixture on the aid circuit.

She's done Rwanda, Congo, Somalia and a short stint in Kosovo, which she didn't much care for. Too close to home.

She sends her Round Robins to all her girlfriends from school and college, who are settled and raising their families.

She wants her life to sound cutting-edge, exotic and meaningful.

She has been out of Britain for so long because she's a misfit whenever she goes back.

Besides, she has a thing about African men.

Tent 27, South Camp,
Save the World Outreach Programme,
Zomba,
Malawi

Dear All

Well, here I am again – back at last in the dark heart of the dark
continent – this Christmas I will be celebrating in Malawi – good thing
for me – Iraqis just don't do it for me, nor indeed did life in Colchester
and the DFID desk job.

I've been sent here with a new NGO, the Save The World
Outreach (STWO) programme, to rescue any Sudanese refugees who
decide to make the 2,000-km trek down through Kenya, Tanzania and
Mozambique. None have done that – yet – and I was a little bit
surprised that STWO thought any would come this far – but in Africa
I've learned always to expect the unexpected.

Besides, it's so wonderful to be hands-on again with these tall,
muscular men – though once again through such desperately tragic
circumstances, of course. If any children ever turn up at our camp,
they will probably have been walking for days and will almost
certainly be dangerously dehydrated. Coca Cola has sponsored an
oral rehydration programme, and we have a healthy stockpile of rice
flown in weekly by UNHCR – along with our supplies of essentials like
Head n Shoulders and Cosmopolitan. There's healthy competition
among the NGOs in Zomba to get any refugees first – a German
Lutheran organisation here is often up before sunrise to be the first to
find anyone looking lost and hungry – so we've started sending Jeep
parties out at midnight to scour the jungle for any that may come
along. It means getting up early – but it will be worth it if there are
people to help.

We have a DDG (drop-dead gorgeous!) 6'4" X'longa tribal
Sudanese called N'djanga arranging the distribution for us. I helped
him unload 25,000 buckets for the proposed sanitation programme
last week – enough for half a million refugees if they ever come –
which took us well past nightfall, we were having such a giggle, and a
few beers later – after the job was done – life was great! The spirit,
humour and sheer passion of the Africans make me feel so alive! Here
are these people who have so little and still have so much love to give

– it puts my own 38 years on this needy Earth in so much perspective – and makes me realise it's not about possessions or being settled – it's about relationships and people. Here I still feel I can make a difference – they need me. I was sorry to miss all those weddings over the summer – I'm still not very good at them after what happened with Malcolm – and besides, duty called!

N'djanga says he wants to take me back to his village up north in Mzuzu to meet his parents. It's amazing how close people can become so quickly in the middle of a crisis – the normal rules of engagement break down and intense relationships spring up overnight. I'm excited to be invited into his part of Africa – and to see his family as an equal – not as a western development worker. I'm not sure whether he'd fit in Colchester, though.

While we wait for refugees, STWO has flown me up to Nairobi in October for the regional Aid and Development Conference. A lot of the usual UNHCR crowd was there and Sir Bob – or The Great Unwashed as everyone calls him – made his traditional guest speech. I hooked up with my old friend M'weta from Congo days with the CORP. He's still as wild he was when we were evacuated during the civil war, and we took the bus down to Malindi on the coast for our R&R. We had a great time pottering about on old Arab dhows and lazing on the beach watching the sun set – and rise!!

Have a great Christmas and enjoy the turkey – my Christmas lunch looks like pizza from the Camp Stone Oven Company – an enterprising lot these Malawians, and they get a good crisp crust too – and mealie meal. We've got some beers and champagne flown in from UNHCR in Dar es Salaam (there's not a drop to be had in Blantyre or Lilongwe) – and N'djanga and his friends will be around for the festive season – so there should be some good partying out here in the bush.

Do write – the bush telegraph takes a while but I love getting your letters whenever the weekly supply plane gets through.

Go well and stay well – as they say in Soweto.

Much love,

Claire

THE EX-MEMBER OF PARLIAMENT

Piers Witherbottom (MA Cantab, OBE, MBA) may have trouble with the voters, but he has no problems with self- confidence. He has a skin that would impress the average rhinoceros.

He has lost his Woodbridge South seat and has fallen back on his old business of coaching public speakers and managing charitable and financial projects.

He is a man convinced of his own value to humanity, and fortunately, has a complete lack of self-awareness.

Further proof of this is the recent departure of Ellen, his wife of fifteen years. She didn't leave him for another man – she just left him.

He sends his Round Robins to business associates and friends who he wants to invest in his new ventures. Well, it beats working.

Piers Witherbottom (MA Cantab, OBE, MBA).
A review of the year's activities.

With my customary humility I say that it's been a difficult year for me in many ways. A lot of my noble efforts have been frustrated. But as those of you who have supported me through thick and thin (we who know "They" should never have got the first term in office, let alone the second and Lord help us all if they get a third!), know I am not a man to be beaten. I see disaster as another word for opportunity, and I have wasted no time in grasping those that come along.

Politics

As I am sure the many of you who have assiduously followed my glittering Parliamentary career will be sadly aware the Party saw an upset when I was pipped at the post to lose my seat by a slender margin of 34,672 votes. It was with some disappointment that I got the lowest number of votes after all my dedication and commitment, then irritation when I saw the frankly abysmal calibre of the successful candidate. You will be pleased to hear, though, that I firmly intend to do all I can to help my constituency and my people from the outside.

Business

I have returned to running my highly popular and successful Public Speakers' Courses. (See www.johnbull_talking.com.) With my lengthy experience in Parliament I offer cutting-edge speaker skills training for all those who have what it takes to achieve great things in public life. I can't recommend these courses too highly, if you or your staff haven't yet benefited from them. Knowing how to present yourself and your business is invaluable in this day and age. I am continually amazed at how incompetent and inarticulate most public servants are and, despite not securing the training contract I had hoped with the Inner London Authority, I continue to try to influence and improve the image of the public sector through privately funded courses.

Having made considerable contacts during my time as a democratically elected Member of Parliament I also recently set up a commercial property company in South London (see http://www.safe_as_houses.com), which secures and sells office space before it comes onto the open market. If you are interested in secure returns, it's something the savvier investors would be well advised to put some money into.

Charity

The multitude of worthy projects I am involved in continue to change lives for the better. (See www.deals_on_wheels.org for just some of the sterling work I've been doing for the handicapped.) I've spent a lot of time giving (free) advice to so many organisations and individuals, and I am sure they get value for money from it. I also managed a fact-finding mission to Mauritius in April. This was such an eye-opener and very humbling. I recommend everyone should visit this kind of charitable projects to appreciate true poverty. I sent my report to UNESCO but they did not seem very interested. Nevertheless, I am sure my recommendations will find themselves into an

international initiative in the near future, such is my expertise and reputation from my years in Parliament. I also had a well-written and fascinating article turned down by the Independent and National Geographic, but I am hopeful its merits will be appreciated by one of the hundreds of other publications I have sent it to. Watch out for my name in print!

Personal

Some of you may also have heard from Ellen that we are no longer together. She was a fine companion, but at the end of the day she lacked the commitment and vision to stay with me and contribute to the greater good. I wish her well in her loneliness.

I sign off wishing you all Health, Wealth and Happiness, an excellent trio of things to have in life! And remember, I am here when you need advice.

Best regards

**Piers Witherbottom
(MA Cantab, OBE, MBE)**

THE ARTISTIC SINGLE MOTHER

Becky Aldridge juggles her life.

Now 31, she works as a costume designer for a small community theatre in North London.

She supplements her income with adult education evening classes for people with special needs, and she lives with her ten-year-old daughter Flora in an old Georgian house, which has been broken up into flats.

Flora's father, Winston Abagula, is an actor. When he is not in rep with the Royal Shakespeare Company, he lives with his new partner, Gideon.

They often visit Becky and Flora for Sunday lunch and a 'family' walk.

Becky and Flora send their Round Robins – this year done in the style of theatre programme biographies – inside cards they hand-make together on their old kitchen table.

Becky Aldridge was last seen in the late-night crowd-pleaser, *Rushing Round Asda*, where she played an overworked mother stocking up for Christmas at 4am. Still making her way as a costume designer, this year Becky has designed grunge outfits for disillusioned teenagers in *Get us Out of Here*, a community play about the education system; and the pink vinyl costumes for *The Mahogany and The Ecstasy* an experimental piece about racism and drugs. She also can be seen sewing tie-dyed boxer shorts for the leading men in her life, Winston and Gideon, for their matching, hand-embroidered Christmas stockings.

Becky trained in childcare, teaching and costume design. This year she has created a routine which just allows an early evening interval with her leading lady, Flora. Taking a role in an improv two-hander with the versatile and talented Mrs Macallister, (the old dear downstairs at No 2a), Becky has dug deep to produce a fine performance of maternal attention, meals and playtime. With some regret, she turned down a supporting part in *Keeping the House Spick and Span* and instead plays the lead in *Organised Chaos*.

Her credits on the small screen include roles in *Yoga, In the Park*, and as supporting actress to Flora in *School Days*. Her interests include steam baths at the local health co-operative, parent teacher meetings and redecorating the mildew-infested avocado bathroom as an underwater mermaid grotto with 3D starfish and embossed shells – insisted on by her leading lady.

Becky is currently wearing too many hats in *The Pantomime of Life*. The script keeps changing, and sometimes, when the house lights go down, she wonders if she's losing the plot.

Flora Abagula trained in the Three Rs at Hackney High Primary School where she caught the eye of the critics for her role in *Fun and Mischief*. A talented comedienne, singer, dancer and all-round star, Flora's performance in *Rainbows* left us all spellbound and it has led to her getting a part in the long-running show, *Girl Guides*. She makes regular guest appearances on *Multi-Faith Assembly* as the third recorder from the left.

A dab hand with a paintbrush, her constant creations cover the myriad cracks in the kitchen paintwork, and can also be seen in the private collection of the well-known patron of the arts, Mrs Macallister downstairs. She has performed many times this year in *Long Leafy Walks* and the musical comedy *She'll Be Riding Her Old Pink Barbie Bicycle When She Comes* along the disused railway cycle path, with the highly acclaimed screen heart-throbs Winston and Gideon.

Off-stage, Flora is an avid collector of small ceramic animals and she aspires to be the first hamster owner in 15 Goldwell Gardens. Her hobbies include nail biting, which she promises will finish its run next year, making handmade beads from paper-mache, and watching unsuitable TV programmes whenever she's at No 2a.

She is a happy, creative and cheeky little companion and I don't know what I would do without her.

A Merry Christmas to you all!

THE HIGH-MAINTENANCE WIFE

Portia is perfect.

Her 45-year-old skin is smooth and flawless, thanks to generous libations with Crème de la Mer, and a discreet little surgeon just off Harley Street.

Not a single Nicky-Clarke-coiffed hair dares stray out of place.

She married Archie Porter, who indulges her because he lacks the imagination to think of anything better to spend his City bonuses on.

They have one son, Charles, fifteen – at Eton, of course – and houses in Kensington, Wiltshire and Verbier.

Portia's background was modest, and as a result her husband's immense wealth has gone to her head, displacing very little when it got there.

Her Round Robins are embossed on rolled parchment tied with a silk ribbon, and delivered in hand-made boxes to all the other banking wives, just in case they forget how obscenely wealthy and stylish she is.

Darlings,

It's that time again, when I so come into my own. Bond Street is my playground, London is so blissfully tempting, and I have such fun buying it up. Christmas is my most favourite time of year, when darling Archie fills my stocking with such divine things from Tiffany's.

This year Archie suggested I might do something more than shopping (the very idea!) and that a little bit of charity work would befit my role as wife of a future Lord Mayor. But, my dears, what can I do? Everyone else is doing cripples and war zones. Besides, I had just given half my wardrobe to Clothes for Africa. Those Somali women have such _divinely_ slim figures and that lovely dusky skin, they were born to wear Ferragamo, and I don't expect they mind it being last season's, do they?

So instead I thought those darling donkeys, which get so maltreated by those _ghastly_ Europeans, were just so deserving. So we held a gloriously lavish black-tie fund-raising jolly at the Dorchester for the Donkey Sanctuary, and I donated all the orchids from our hothouse in Wiltshire. Those poor deserving donkeys now have a luxurious sanctuary in Guernsey, which they simply insisted I should have it named after me, so Portia's Grooming Room it is! I do so feel I have made a difference to their suffering, because I know how much better one feels when one's hair is properly done. Perhaps next year I shall set up a travelling hair-salon in Africa. When I see them on the television, I'm always astonished that they've made _so_ little effort. Archie is frightfully proud of my endeavors. It does make one want to give more.

Archie says I should get a hobby to keep me busy, but I find that shopping really is a serious commitment and keeps me so busy. Each Prada Moment is quite exhausting! I simply had to have all their new handbags and shoes. And, my dears, there was the latest must-have pink satin Burberry trench. Archie says perhaps pink is not quite my colour so I bought all the lime green as well, which he said was far more me. Darlings, their new range is _so_ sumptuous. I have also been updating our little country retreat, and had this sweet new interior designer Riccardo Sparchesi, who picked up this year's House and Gardens award, do up the guest wing. Archie wanted something more late Tudor, but anti-modernist urban brutalism is just so _in_. You really must come and stay.

And, oh! What another hectic year! All this living for pleasure is quite exhausting! Verbier beckoned twice, and we took Charlie and his royal friend (whom I think some of you may know!) out of school for a week. I bought a fabulous Norwegian Pisterekka snowboard for Charlie, and a matching one for Archie. It's hanging on the wall in the library in Wiltshire, as he felt it was not quite his scene, but he _does_ like the look of it. We cruised the summer away around the BVI on Portia's Palazzo, the darling little 63-footer you may remember Archie bought me for my big birthday a few years ago. Quite exhausting! So to revive me, Archie sends me away every month to La Retraite where I always instruct them to fly over the therapists from the Twin Toners in New York, as they're the only ones who _really_ understand my skin.

Soon Charlie will be home from Eton and we can head down to the country. It's always so lovely to deck one's halls with boughs of holly one's own staff has gathered from one's own land. Charlie does so love to be with Wuffers again, too, and to take one of the thoroughbreds out for a gallop for a few hours around a small corner of the estate.

Must dash as my personal masseur will pop round any minute and then I have to squeeze in my mani and pedi before meeting Archie at The Ivy for our weekly supper a deux.

Have a simply _heavenly_ Christmas. Hope that Santa brings you Tiffany too. All our love, darlings

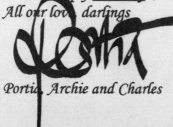

Portia, Archie and Charles

THE LOTTERY-WINNING CHAVS

Trish and Des got one thing right in their lives. They picked six numbers.

Before that, Trish had left school at sixteen and was working in a newsagents. She met Des at ladies night at Foxxxies nightclub in Dagenham.

Des is 25, and reckons himself a man of the world after a few years in the army and a tour of duty in Cyprus.

They are having a laugh spending their winnings, and they don't give a damn what people think of them.

This is their first Round Robin, and they're sending it to remind everyone how rich they are, and what fun it is to spend like there's no tomorrow.

HUGE MANSION
ROMFORD
ESSEX

DEAR ALL,

ANYONE WHAT TELLS YOU MONEY DON'T BUY YOU HAPPINESS DIDN'T WIN ENOUGH OF IT IS ALL WE CAN SAY. WE'RE HAVING AN ACE TIME WITH WHAT DES GOT OFF THE LOTTERY AND YOU CAN TAKE IT FROM ME WHAT WE'RE DOING WITH THE DOSH IS FANTASTIC!!! GOOD THING WE DIDN'T HAVE TO SHARE IT WITH NO ONE BECAUSE WHEN YOU COME DOWN TO IT £18,768,940 DON'T BUY YOU AS MUCH AS WHAT IT SHOULD DO. DES SAYS IT'S BECAUSE OF LABOUR BEING IN.

WHAT'S REALLY GREAT IS THAT DES AND ME HASN'T CHANGED NOTHING AND WERE STILL LIVING HERE IN BECKENHAM AFTER ALL ITS HOME AND IF YOU HAVEN'T GOT YOUR MATES AROUND YOU WHAT HAVE YOU GOT? HE'S STILL GOT HIS OLD JOB AT THE BUILDERS MERCHANTS, ONLY HE DON'T GO IN AS MUCH AS HE USED TO LIKE NOT EVERY DAY BECAUSE HE DON'T REALLY NEED THE MONEY BUT HE LIKES TO SEE HIS MATES.

WE GOT THIS NEW PLACE BUILT THOUGH BECAUSE WE NEED MORE SPACE WHAT WITH THE QUAD BIKE TRACK DES GOT BECAUSE HE ALWAYS LIKED A BURN UP AFTER ALL, AND MY BORZOIS NEED A LOT OF SPACE TO RUN AROUND IN AND DES SAID HE WANTS TO PUT IN AN ADVENTURE PLAYGROUND FOR WHEN WE HAVE KIDS AND FOR HIS MATES TO HAVE A LAUGH ON NOW.

DES GOT A SWIMMING POOL PUT IN TOO ALTHOUGH WE HAD TO KNOCK DOWN A COUPLE OF THE TERRACES NEXT DOOR AND ONE OF THEM HAD THIS FAMILY WHAT DIDN'T WANT TO MOVE OUT SO WE GOT THE BOYS IN AND SORTED THEM GOOD. DES GOT THIS WAY COOL HI-FI FROM MINISTRY OF SOUND, IT'S SECOND HAND BUT WHEN IT'S CRANKED UP YOU CAN REALLY FEEL THE BASS IT'S LIKE THE WHOLE STREET SHAKES, IT'S WICKED. WE GOT A PERSONAL TRAINER MIKHAIL WHO

DONE ARSENAL LAST SEASON SO HE MUST BE ALLRIGHT AND HE IS DOING GREAT WITH ME BECAUSE YOU GOT TO HAVE THE FIGURE TO CARRY OFF LEOPARD SKIN TROUSERS, LIKE MY NEW FRIEND VICTORIA BECKHAM WAS TELLING ME WHEN ME AND HER WAS DRINKING VODKA REDBULLS IN HER HOUSE THE OTHER DAY AND SHE SHOULD KNOW SHOULDN'T SHE?

WE DID A REALLY GREAT PARTY FOR MY BIRTHDAY OVER THE SUMMER, WELL YOU'RE ONLY 17 ONCE, SO WE REALLY WENT FOR IT, WE GOT ROBBIE WILLIAMS TO COME ALONG AND SING, HE'S A BORN ENTERTAINER ISN'T HE AND HE'S ALWAYS GOOD TO MAKE A PARTY GO WITH A BANG ALTHOUGH VICTORIA WAS NARKED HOW SHE WASN'T ASKED TO SING. IT WAS ACE, WE WAS SO WELLIED ME AND SOME OF THE GIRLS DID A SHOW FOR THE BOYS SO ME AND DES HAD TO GO ROUND AND GET ALL THE TAPES OUT OF THE SECURITY CAMERAS WE DON'T WANT TO END UP ON THE INTERNET DO WE!?!

WE GOT THIS GREAT ROLLER FROM A MATE OF DES'S WHAT SELLS CARS HE SAID IT BELONGED TO SNOOP DOGGY DOG IT'S REALLY WICKED WITH GOLD TAPS WITH CHAMPAGNE IN THEM AND EVERYTHING, A PLASMA TV AND DVD AND LIKE A STEREO WITH 10 SPEAKERS, WE HAD THE SEATS DONE IN ZEBRA SKIN BECAUSE SNOOP IS LIKE FROM AFRICA ISN'T HE? WE GOT A PARKING TICKET WHEN WE WAS SHOPPING FOR PRADA ON BOND STREET THOUGH, STUPID IDIOTS DON'T THEY KNOW A ROLLER WHEN THEY SEE ONE?!?

SOME THINGS HAVE CHANGED THOUGH LIKE LAST YEAR WE GOT 10 XMAS CARDS AND NO ONE GIVE US NOTHING BUT THIS YEAR WE GOT LIKE OVER 200 BEGGING XMAS CARDS AND PEOPLE WAS ALL QUEUING UP FROM THE BEGINNING OF NOVEMBER GIVING US ALL STUFF, WHICH IS A LAUGH REALLY BECAUSE IT'S NOT LIKE WE NEED IT NOW IS IT? WE EVEN GOT A FUNNY LETTER AND XMAS CARD FROM THE BANK SAYING AS HOW WE HAD SPENT ALL WHAT THE LOTTERY GIVE US, THEY MUST BE HAVING A LAUGH RIGHT!? ANYWAY YOU'RE ALL INVITED TO OUR BIG XMAS PARTY WHAT OUR ACCOUNTANT HAS TOLD US TO HAVE IN MAY BECAUSE OF TAX BREAKS SO WERE GONNA DO SANTA IN BIKINIS WITH A WET STOCKING TOP COMPETITION AND EVERYTHING, ITS GONNA BE LUSH SEE YOU THERE!!!!

LOVE

TRISH AND DES

THE TRAVELLING RETIREES

Since they retired at 55, Bella and Roddy Walker have had to get new passports every three years, as the pages fill up so fast.

Inseparable, they have been round the world a dozen times in the last ten years.

They have no children.

Roddy made his money with a few good property deals in the 80s, and Bella ran an upmarket florist in Wilmslow.

They often travel in matching Birkenstocks and those Craghoppers Kiwi pants which unzip at the knee to become shorts, with collapsible sunhats in their pockets.

They have a large group of equally rich, equally well-travelled friends, and they all swap holiday stories in their Round Robins.

54 Tudor Court, Congleton, Cheshire

Dear All,

In haste, as we are off for a few days' jolly across the Channel to buy our festive fizz from our favourite vineyard near Epernay and I want to get our cards in the post before we go. No surprises that we've been packing in our usual holidays-of-a-lifetime every few months – a perk of our retirement – although this year ours have been extra-special, of course.

January saw us leaving behind winter's chill for three weeks' bird-watching in Thailand. Stayed in a gorgeous hideaway in the beautifully russet-tinged, teak-forested hills around Chiang Rai, where magnificent asian fairy bluebirds, racket-tailed drongos and golden orioles flitted through the lush, verdant tropical canopy. We enjoyed blissfully hot days and nights, and mouth- and eye-watering cuisine, although Roddy had to take it easy on the "zingier" dishes.

March was our usual fortnight at Schloss Palmer, Neethia and Teddy's place in the Tirol, for crisp, new, white snow, wonderful skiing and our usual rowdy crowd. We travelled back through France where spring had come early, covering the Haute Savoie with a rich mantle of blossoms and wildflowers. We spent a glorious couple of weeks in the mountains above Chambery and took our favourite route up to our regular little auberge, Maison d'Envoi, with our beloved views over Mount Blanc. We had fabulous, golden weather and spent glorious, tranquil, sun-filled days on the terrace sipping our wine in dappled sunshine. The soothing sound of birdsong and the humming of bees added to our ambience of relaxation and rest. Roddy got quite misty-eyed when we drove away, as "our" Maison has always been filled with special memories.

In June we were back in the UK and we did a most pleasurable week's tour of National Trust Gardens, staying in some divine Wolsey

Lodges. Once again we had fabulous weather and marvelled at the cascading lilac wisteria at Sissinghurst, fed the frisky oriental carp in the Japanese Gardens at Cliveden and celebrated our 35th wedding anniversary there in the luxurious Lady Astor Suite, with such impeccable, charming service and Michelin-starred cuisine.

After such a low-key summer we decided to hang the expense, and to visit the Great Wall of China. Roddy has never forgiven himself for not sailing on the Yangtze before they flooded it, so we bit the proverbial bullet and flew to Beijing. We found the Wall breathtakingly splendid, a glorious monument to man's achievement. Even though we were amazed to see it's so dilapidated in parts where people are actually taking the stones to build houses with, its noble grandeur made a huge impact on us both. We came back on the Trans-Siberian Express, something we've always wanted to do, and one of the world's great journeys, which lived up to all our expectations.

In October, Roddy declared he felt up to his usual sailing jolly in Turkey with his old workmates, so I had a few days with my old friend Sophie in the much raved-about new spa at Heartwell House. Indulged in this wonderful new treatment where they pass an anodysed neutral current, tuned in with your own natural bio-rhythms, through your body, and came out feeling slimmer and years younger. We met up in Vienna to see the stunning performance of Der Rosenkavalier at the Opera House, something we'd always promised ourselves

Roddy was back at the Royal Marsden for more tests in November – thank goodness for Bupa – and the specialist gave him an OK, certainly for a few more months. So we are looking forward to a few more holidays-of-a-lifetime together in the early months of next year. Angkor Wat, a Namibian safari, Petra, Roddy says there is still so much to see, although he's realistic enough to know we won't see it all.

Hope all is well with you. Do come and see us if you are passing. Roddy always loves to see his old friends.

Lots of love,

Bella & Roddy

THE TRENDY MEDIA COUPLE

Johnno Adams and Miranda Smithers live in Hoxton in a high-ceilinged first-floor flat.

Just 30, Johnno is in advertising and Miranda, who kept her maiden name, is running her own one-man financial PR agency.

They have an eighteen-month-old daughter, Apple, who wears all the latest Osh Kosh and Life Baby outfits and accessories. She has been brought up by an unreliable string of highly paid foreign nannies.

Johnno and Miranda enjoy all that London offers – and they can afford to.

Miranda is hoping her Round Robin will bring in some more business.

MEDIA ALERT!!!

Johnno Adams and Miranda Smithers announce record levels of fun last year.

Well-known media darlings Johnno Adams and Miranda Smithers today released figures showing an unprecedented level of jollity, good cheer and amusement for the past year. A substantial programme of investment in parties, holidays, dinners and theatre visits has yielded a better-than-average performance. Their stock, already pegged at 2,245 on the FTSE100 (Fantastic Times Social Exchange 100) looks set to rise even further and break the 2,500 mark.

Johnno said: "This year will go down as a record year in terms of us having a good time. We hope that shareholders in our fun and fashion-filled lifestyle choice will continue to support us as we party on down into next year! Based on vital signs, economic indicators and what I've got in my PDA for January and February alone, we anticipate even higher levels of happiness ahead."

His partner Miranda added: "The year has also seen a high level of investment of time and energy into launching my new financial PR company, Real Financial Sense, which is currently in the market for new clients. We offer a tailor-made programme of fully interactive media liaison, specialising in web design, viral marketing and buzz tactics, which will ensure your brand is kept in the public eye where it belongs. "Our fee structure is highly competitive with companies offering similar services," she added.

realfinancialensefifteencharliesnowmewshoxtonlondon
tel+44(0)20777777 fax+44(0)20888888emailmiranda@realfinancialsense.co.uk

Minority shareholder Apple Adams–Smithers has been one of the principal beneficiaries of the high levels of investment in fun. She has seen her holdings in Osh Kosh, Baby Gap and Barbie soar, particularly during her birthday. She is planning to diversify her holdings into Bratz and Boyz dolls at Christmas, has significant futures options in Stocks R Us, and she continues to single-handedly boost Disney Videos' share price. Some senior members of the Board, Grandma and Grandpa Adams, said: "Apple is so cute. We will be cashing in some of our pension funds to make sure she has a Christmas to remember."

Highlights of the couple's annual report include:

- Johnno turning 30, and taking 30 friends to Babington House
- Seeing our hedge fund portfolio break the five-year record
- Investing in an original Alison Lapper for the living area
- Selling our Citroen DS convertible to Charles Saatchi
- Saturday latte at Dell'Olio, while Apple draws on the tablecloth
- Designing Zoe Wannamaker's dress for Peter Hall's new Happy Days
- Sending Apple to Mozart Lamaze classes at the Design Centre
- Hang-gliding over Machu Picchu without oxygen

Some investments did not return the expected dividends however, and Johnno and Miranda took the hard decision to divest themselves of their holding in Bertha The Lazy Fat East German Childminder Gmbh, after her stock fell dramatically in the second quarter. This followed hard on the heels of a similar under-performing shares in Shireen The Unreliable Australian Slapper Ltd, but at least the recent sale has released funds to invest in Olga The Hard Working But Ugly Slovak Nanny Plc, a recent eastern European start-up.

Issued on behalf of Johnno Adams and Miranda Smithers by Real Financial Sense PR. For interviews, promotional appearances or parties, Johnno and Miranda can be contacted at: 15 Charlie Snow Mews, Hoxton, London. E-mail: miranda@realfinancialsense.com Tel: +44 (0) 20 777 7777. Fax: +44 (0) 20 888 8888.

---

realfinancialsensefifteencharliesnowmewshoxtonlondon
tel+44(0)20777777 fax+44(0)20888888emailmiranda@realfinancialsense.co.uk

THE NEW WIDOW

Bertie Trentham died quite suddenly while tending his allotment.

Now his widow Agnes is trying to come to terms with the empty space he has left in her life. At 72, her life had always revolved around Bertie and the children.

She lives in the scrupulously spick and span bungalow Bertie bought for their retirement.

A polite and unassuming woman, Agnes has never lived on her own before.

She sends her Round Robins to her and Bertie's old friends, as well as a couple of cousins who are now in Australia.

Dear All

It is with great sadness that I write this Xmas
as this is the first year I will be spending it
without my dear Bertie who lost his fight with
cancer this summer passing away two months before
our Ruby Wedding Anniversary, such a shame and I
had to cancel the special lunch we had booked at
our local hotel, The Grange. Still everyone got
together for the funeral and the dear Reverend
Julian Petty did a wonderful service with the
Hymns which we had at our Wedding my dear friend
Mavis did wonderful Flowers for the Church and
The Grange did us a good four-star spread for the
wake with a nice rice salad and Scotch eggs which
I know my dear Bertie would have enjoyed.

Mavis has been a great support and I managed
to get through the Autumn helping her out with
the Bingo at the local Hospital and the Xmas
Bazaar for Cancer Relief I'm also very grateful
for the company of my television as those dark
evenings drew in although I do miss that funny
Michael Barrymore. Evelyn came for a few days to
help with her Dad's funeral and was a tower of
strength it's a shame she had to go back the day

after but I know how the children keep her busy
and I'm sure she was right that they're too young
to understand what's happened to poor dear
Grandpa. I wouldn't want to spoil their Xmas,
either.

We were all sorry that Greg was not able to
make it back from Canada for his poor Dad's
funeral due to work commitments and is going
skiing somewhere smart in the USA this Christmas
and Evelyn is busy with the in-laws in Yorkshire
this year so I am not quite sure what I will be
doing on Xmas Day, I am not sure whether to go to
The Grange for Xmas Lunch or order Meals on
Wheels and watch the Queen's Speech. Mavis always
goes away to her son in Brighton over the Xmas
Period, but she has said she will phone in the
morning, which is nice of her. She has been such
a dear friend in this sad time.

Still I am sure you will all have a happy
family time this Festive Season and may I wish
you all a very Merry Xmas and a Happy New Year. I
will be thinking of you all - and of my dear
Bertie - at this Festive Time

With warmest wishes,

Agnes

Agnes

THE LONDON WORKING GIRL

Jane Jenkins is not really a City girl.

She's a farmer's daughter from Cheshire, but she's in London to snap up a rich husband.

She's 28, and she's kissing a lot of frogs in order to find her Prince Charming.

But the reality is, she's the kind of dependable, fall-back girl dentists marry when they reach their late 30s.

Her last four Round Robins have all been the same, so this year she's trying to hide the fact that nothing has changed in the last five years.

Diary of a Working Girl,
(or Sex and the City and Plain Jane)

TIME 8,760 hours, which breaks down into:
<u>Working</u>: **2,250** hours, still at The Building Partnership, still PA to Mike Summers, who's still the sales director, still a dish, and still doesn't have a clue how I feel about him. That's **973** hours at the keyboard, **490** on the phone, **192** photocopying, **158** hours collecting Mike's laundry, **40** having lunch with Jenna, **265** having lunch alone at my desk, **132** in the toilet crying, and **2,250** wishing I didn't have to work at all.

<u>Beauty sleep</u>: **2,190** (hmmm, still not paying the dividends I'd like! Nose still same shape, hair still too curly, and eyes still too small).

<u>Ugly sleep</u>: **58** (with David, what a waste of time he turned out to be!)

<u>Good parties</u>: **140** (inc. the New Year's Eve Trafalgar Square Memory Wipe).

<u>Bad parties</u>: **326** (no thanks to a certain David Asquith)

<u>Hot dates</u>: **140** (naming no names – but not booking any churches yet, either!)

<u>Cold dates</u>: **680** (inc. freezing out Jefferson the American Banker, Monty the Lawyer, sweet, hopeless Quentin, Dull David and that sweaty little bald man in the Mr Buyrite suit who stalked me over the summer).

<u>Shopping well</u>: **1,430** (when Harvey Nicks goes 24-hour, you'll see that number *rise*!).

<u>Shopping badly</u>: **8** (can there really be bad shopping? Oh, I think so – when it's buying birthday presents for Mike's wife…).

<u>Eating</u>: **1,198** (that's **258** on the Atkins Diet, **120** on the Glycaemic Index Diet, **217** on Calorie Counters, **125** on Slimfast, **22** on Weight Watchers and **456** on chocolate, burgers, buns and One Is Fun! microwave meals.)

<u>City Slickers Health Club</u>: **260**. That's **103** on the step trainer, **68** on the rowing trainer, **25** on the weight trainer, and **10** under the personal trainer.
<u>Sex</u>: Thinking about it: **300**. Doing it: **98** (memo to self – must work on those numbers!)

MONEY £28,000, which went on:
<u>To Mrs O'Leary</u> (the Evil Landlady From Hell) for the pokiest flat in Balham: **£11,000**
<u>To the taxman</u> (well, *someone* has to keep the NHS afloat): **£5,400**
<u>To Ken Livingstone</u> (who got my vote *before* he scrapped double-deckers) **£600**.
<u>To Happy Daze</u>, still the coolest bar in Islington: **£2,670**. That breaks down into **£2,120** on margaritas, **£342** on vodka menthol frappes, and **£208** on chardonnay and sympathy.
<u>To Coffee Colombia</u> (**£5.30** a cup, but I just *have* to have that buzz in the morning. I wonder if they put something extra in it?): **£1,272**
<u>On lunch from M&S</u>: **£960**
<u>Good investments</u> (inc. the Monty-catching red Victoria's Secret slinky): **£2,495**
<u>Bad investments</u> (inc. the Seventies revival orange-and-purple hotpants): **£129.99**
Cheap fortnight in Ibiza (inc. single traveller surcharge): **£899**
<u>Essentials</u> (inc. Elle, Vogue, foundation, mascara, lipgloss, no-run tights, Angel-crème moisturiser, manicure, Diet Coke, yoghurt, Nurofen, strawberry body-butter, Optimax honey-blonde highlights, weekly leg-wax, Frizz-Ease, Prozac): **£2,574.01**

Happy Christmas, and roll on next year – my sixth year in London.
But, hey, who's counting?
Hugs and kisses,

THE BREATHLESS NEWLYWEDS

Lilith and Reufus Oakengrove were made for each other.

They are blissfully, devotedly, besottedly in love, and will remain so until the gods are thrown from Asgard and the great serpent brings the end of this world and ushers in the dawn of the next.

They are children of the Earth, and a lot of it still clings to them, especially under their fingernails. They tend to wear purple, and have embraced the tassel as a fashion statement.

They were married in a field of cows, although they did pop in to the register office, to keep Reufus's grandmother happy.

Reufus is a poet, Lilith teaches. They send their Round Robins to their family, friends from the folk music circle, and the people they see every year at Cambridge Folk Festival and Glastonbury.

They adore children because they are children.

They will sail through life on a cloud of love and happiness.

Faerie Bower,
Bathamptonwickstead,
Avon

Dear All,

What can we say, except thank you! Thank you all for
your love and well wishes that made our wedding day so memorable!
Thank you Dadi, for officiating! You looked magnificent in your
white robes and your long flowing grey beard, and the oakleaf crown
Mumi made for you was so majestic! And thank you Miranda,
Cordelia, Tanya and little Blossom, who made the sweetest pixie
bridesmaids any girl could wish for. Thanks to Rowena and
Madeleine for decorating the enchanted grove so exquisitely, and to
Odin for playing the flute. The union of Man and Woman is such a
mystical, sacred act, and our marriage vows were the most solemn and
yet sensual moment of our lives. Thank you all for being there.

The honeymoon was a true magical mystical tour, in a
lovely horse-drawn painted caravan (well, a VW camper – thanks,
Odin!) and we drove round the prettiest parts of the Forest of Arden,
parked in fields to watch the sun set, and I confess we tested the
suspension a lot!

Being married is more magical than either of us could have
ever dreamed of. It's almost spiritual how much more in love Reufus
and I become with each and every passing day, and I feel we're just
stepping out on our journey of love, side by side, arm in arm and ♡
to ♡. And having all of you there to wish us well on our special
day brought together a whole community of love around us, lifting us
on white swans' wings us in our joyful spirit-union.

I know Mumi is worried about us "living on fresh air," but
we just know we will be happy. Reufus's poetry has reached new

heights of lyricism — he's so gorgeously talented! The Earl of Bathamptonwickstead was so impressed with his first volume, "Tales of Olde and Sails of Golde", he's agreed to be Reufus's patron, and has given us the sweetest tumbledown cottage in a secret corner of his estate. It's true that if you believe in the beauty of people, magical things will happen for you!

While I teach at the local primary, where the children are just so sweet, Reufus is at home baking bread and tending our organic garden. When I come home and find the house full of the smell of fresh-baked bread, and him with earth on his great big hands, he's irresistible! I know Mumi didn't really like Reufus's big red beard at first, but I think it's just scrummy! We started making babies almost as soon as we got through the door, because Reufus and I agree it's important to fill the world with tiny happy people. Sometimes I lie in Reufus's arms as the morning sun streams through our little cottage windows, and he reads me his newest poem, and we're so happy we giggle ourselves silly. We've painted our bedroom a rich purple, which looks glorious with the tapestries Morgana gave us for a wedding present. In the evenings, I'm embroidering a waistcoat for Reufus, while he writes by candlelight for inspiration.

The silkies Wykeham gave us are scratching happily in the yard. We couldn't bear to tear them away from any of their eggs, and there are now almost 40 of them, so if anyone wants a gorgeous little chicken (as a pet!), please let us know.

Reufus has just brought in the Yule log from the forest, and has made a bough of holly, ivy and pine branches to hang over the mantel, which smells so delicious mixed with the sweet scent of warm mead. Magic is in the air!

With all our hearts' love this Yuletide season,

Lilith and Reufus.

Lot #189,
CRIPPLE CREEK MOBILE RESIDENCES ZONE 23,
JUNCTION CITY,
ARKANSAS, USA

HI Y'ALL,

WE SURELY DO MISS ALL OUR GOOD BUDDIES IN LONDON ENGLAND, PARIS FRANCE + BELGIUM EUROPE! MEBBE YOU'RE MISSING YOUR AMERICAN COUSINS, SO HERE'S A CATCH-UP WITH LIFE IN SLEEPY ARKANSAS!

WAYNE JR MADE US ALL REAL PROUD NOW HE'S THE EIGHT IN THIS LI'L FAMILY TO BE ABDUCTED BY ALIENS. IT HAPPENED JUST LIKE GRANPAPPY JOE SAID, THE LIGHTS, THE WIND, THE ANAL PROBE, OUR BOY HAD IT ALL. THEM THERE ALIENS PUMPED HIM FULL OF JACK DANIELS TILL HE COULDN'T HARDLY SEE NONE, THEN DUMPED HIM DOWN IN OLD MA ROBINSON'S '83 CHEVY COUPE ON THE WRONG SIDE OF THE INTERSTATE HIGHWAY DOING 110 PER. AT LEAST, THAT'S WHERE THE STATE TROOPER FOUND HIM.

DARLEENA JR WAS CROWNED MISS CORN DOG ARKANSAS AT THE COUNTY FAIR JULY LAST. SHE MADE ME SO PROUD! ME + HER SPENT ALL THEM HOURS STITCHIN' THEM 4,000 PINK SATEEN BOWS ONTO THAT THERE DRESS OF HERS'N, AND IT JUST PLAIN NOCKED THE JUDGES' SOCKS OFF'N. SHE LOOKED AS CUTE AS MAYBE, JUS' 13 YEARS OLD + GROWN SO BIG. AH CONFESS AH HAD TO WIPE AWAY A TEAR, SHE LOOKED JUS' LIKE THE PRETTY LI'L GIRL AH ONCE WAS BEFORE THE WIEGHT GAIN + THE TATTOOS. SHE CAME HOME WITH THE BIGGEST CRATE OF CORN DOGS YOU EVER DID SEE, PLUS THE CHEQUE FOR $2,000 WHICH AH PUT AWAY SOMEPLACE SAFE FROM WAYNE (IN THE WASHROOM — HE DON'T NEVER GO THERE THESE DAYS!).

ARLON TURNED 12 OVER THE SUMMER + IS ROUND HERE SOMEPLACE, BUT WE AIN'T SEEN HIM NONE SINCE AUGUST, WHEN HE WENT OUT 'GATOR BAITING ON CRIPPLE CREEK. AH EXPECT HE'LL BE BACK FOR CHRISTMAS. HE NEVER

→ MISSES MAH FAMOUS CORN DOG TURKEY POT ROAST.
AND MARLON, WHO'S 11, HE MISSES HIS BROTHER SO, HE AIN'T
NEVER ONCE STEPPED OUT OF HIS ROOM IN ALL THAT TIME.
AH LEAVES A TRAY OF GOOD CORN DOG SOUP BY HIS DOOR EVERY
DAY, AND IT'S ALWAYS GONE BY MORNIN', SO WE FIGURE HE'S DOIN'
FINE, HE JUST NEEDS A LI'L TIME TO HISSELF.

SHARLONA'S GETTIN' BIGGER + BIGGER, WHAT WITH HOW SHE
JUST SITS THERE IN THE CORNER ALL DAY IN THAT BIG EASY CHAIR OF
HERS'N HUMMIN' QUIETLY TO HERSELF LIKE'N SHE ALWAYS DONE SINCE
THE ACCIDENT. REVEREND JOHNSON SAYS HE'S SURE SHE'S FOUND
JESUS, SO WE ~~XXXX~~ JUS' LEAVE HER BE. SOMETIMES AH LIKE TO
SIT WITH HER ALTHOUGH AH DON'T THINK SHE SEES ME NONE,
BUT IT'S KINDA RESTFUL JUS' BEIN' WITH HER.

HER BROTHER HARLON GETS OUT OF JAIL FEBUARY NEXT + ME +
DARLEENA JR, WE'RE GONNA BAKE HIM THE BIGGEST CORN DOG PIE
ARKANSAS EVER SAW. HE LOVES IT SO. WE GOT GOOD CAUSE FOR
A PARTY, 'CAUSE THOSE STATE TROOPERS THEY NEVER DID FIND
HAIR NOR HIDE OF THAT MONEY HARLON STOLE, SO WE GONNA BE LIVIN'
PRETTY IF HE CAN REMEMBER WHERE IT IS.

WAYNE'S GETTIN' WAY TOO BIG FOR THIEVIN' NOW, SO HE'S
DIVERSIFYIN' INTO BLACKMAIL WITH THIS NEW DIGITAL CAMERA OF HIS'N.
FIRST OFF HE SET UP JUDGE WHITE WITH A COUPLE OF FANCY GIRLS OF
A KIND HIS WIFE DON'T NEED TO KNOW ABOUT, AND NOW HE'S GETTIN'
SHERIFF JOHNSON PRESERVED IN PICTURES WITH THAT PRETTY LI'L
HOG OF HIS'N HE'S SO ATTACHED TO.

IF ANY OF YOU FINDS YOURSELF'N IN JUNCTION CITY, DON'T
YOU BE STRANGERS, Y'HEAR?

DARLEENA, WAYNE, WAYNE JR, MARLON, ARLON, HARLON
AND SHARLONA.

THE HYPOCHONDRIAC

Timothy Blenkinsopp never married. The baby of the family, he prefers to stay at home and take care of his old Mum.

He has an interesting and varied selection of ailments to draw upon whenever employment threatens to disturb his comfy life.

He is 53, hugely overweight, and knows more about daytime television than is either healthy or relevant.

His Mum is in a wheelchair but still does all the cooking and cleaning.

14 Spalding Road

Kings Lynn,

Norfolk

Dear All,

   It's been a funny old year. Me and Mum are still in her
flat, because I need someone to look after me with my
problems which haven't been any better this year, I'm sorry
to say. I've been in and out of work, too, because it's
hard finding anything my health will let me to do. The
agency found me a clerk's job in an estate agents, but what
with all the people coming and going through the door,
there was a terrible draft and my lumbago flared up something
dreadful so I had to stop. I got a good job at Burger King
because they give you all the burgers you want, but all that
smoke off the grill s4nt my asthma off the scale and I was
coughing and wheezing all over the shop. I could feel it
putting astrain on my heart, so I had to stop after a week.
Since then I've been on benefits, and Mum's pension helps
too. I'm much better , taking it easy.

   We had a day at Maureen's in the spring when Mum turned
80. Mum says she doesn't get to see the grandchildren as
much as she would like, but all the noise they were making
gave me one of my migraines, so I had to go and lie down.
We had to leave earlyeven though Mum would have liked to
stay for tea. Maureen was understanding. She said if you
haven't got your health, you haven't got anything. How true
that is!

   Maureen invited us to join her and Mike and the kids in
Malta on holiday, but with my ear problems I don't like to
fly. Also, something about airplanes always blocks me and I
can't "go" for days afterwards. And my haemorrhoids play
up something awful from sitting so long. And there's the
worry of thrombosis in my legs. I'm also sure I'm getting a
heart murmur because I get breathless quite quickly on
stairs and suchlike. I took some of Mum's angina pills for
a couple of weeks. Funny thing is, they do her the world of
good, but didn't do a lot for me. I still get twinges.

   Me and Mum had a lovely holiday round Derbyshire.
Mohammed next door lent us this book of all the best B&Bs
and we chose the pick of the bunch, though I say so myself.
You can't beat a full English breakfast to set you up for
the day, although Mum does spill her tea on account of her
Parkinsons. It's lovely in the Peak District, although we
didn't always get the benefit of it what with not getting
out of the car. The wind can be chilly, and I don't want to

take the risk with my arthritis. Also getting Mum's chair
out of the boot is a palaver, and pushing it up all those
hills, I don't thinkn so, not with my sciatica.

I'm still baffling the doctors! I've given up on that
useless Doctor Subraimaniam, who still can't get to the bot-
tom of my illnesses. She says I should lose weight, but Mum
says I'm a fine figure for a man of 53, and you have to
trust your Mum, don't you! Maureen and Mike say they'll come
with the kids for Christmas Day, but I feel a bit of flu
coming on and I may have to cancel. It'll be nicer just to
be Mum and me, with abit of turkey, stuffing, roast potatoes
gravy, pudding, Christmas cake and crackers. I expect we'll
see Maureen in the New Year.

Take care of yourselves,

Timothy (and Mum!)

THE HOUSE-CHURCH EVANGELISTS

Donald and Jeannie Macauliffe left Dundee to set up house churches carrying God's message to anyone who will listen.

They have evangelised in Sheffield and Norfolk, and now are saving Bradford.

Both are neat, precise people, whose tastes run to matching Pringle jumpers, blue trousers with that special factory-outlet cut, and sensible Clarks shoes.

They have two children, Matthew and Mary, whose suffering due to their parents' chosen path is reaching Biblical proportions.

Donald and Jeannie's righteousness (and their rightness) knows no boundaries of creed or colour.

They upset a lot of people, but the bright flame of devotion blinds them – which is probably a blessing.

Dear All,

Or should that be Dear All-eluia? Lord Jesus is in all of us – so Dear All-eluia it is!

Following the great success of our seed churches in Norfolk, the Church has asked us to come to Bradford, where we bring the message of God's Love to everyone, regardless of race, creed or colour, so that they too can be Born Again. We extend our heartfelt thanks to the kind people of the House of Our Lord Church in Kings Lynn, whose divinely led generosity allowed us to move north so very, very swiftly.

Bradford is ready to hear the Good News! We set up our first inter-faith discussion group here in July, and we counted 22 local people, many with turbans and other head coverings it's true, but all called by God's Grace. Unbelievably, some of them actually wanted to talk about their own heathen gods! But we would have none if it! There is little enough time for the One True Lord, so we seized the chance to preach the Matchless Perfection of God's Love. I'm sorry to say eight people walked out. The Evil One's work is never far away in our lives here!

But we know that the seeds we are planting, no matter how poor the soil, will one day bear fruit, and that the bricks that come through our windows are merely the foundation stones of a New Jerusalem, to be built here in Bradford.

Jeannie has set up a Women's Outreach group, which stretches into our very needy community. Many of the women here wear clothes of such garish hues as are an affront to any decent-minded person, and these "saris" reveal so much flesh as can only lead to lasciviousness and sin. So Jeannie has followed her Calling to guide them back to a more wholesome, Christian mode of dress, such as sensible tweed skirts, good worsted stockings and a modest blouse and cardigan.

Mary, now 13, faced a challenging time at school this year where she was being bullied mercilessly for her gentle sharing of her Calling to the Kingdom. Her Faith was greatly tested, but she held up through Prayer and was such a witness to us all. She was able to feel close to her Lord, through her understanding what it feels like to be the outcast, bruised, battered, spat upon, scorned and rejected. We were so proud of her fortitude and faith and praise the Lord for the Spirit he has poured into our beautiful daughter. Her teachers have suggested police protection, but we believe it is important for Mary to dwell among her people, as Our Lord did, no matter how cruel they may be to her.

Matthew, who just turned 17, has been further evidence of God's Calling to us. As some of you know, he has been tempted greatly by the Devil and has been arrested twice for possession and dealing in Ecstasy. He recently spent a spell wrestling with his demons in a rehabilitation centre. We are sure that the Lord has great plans for him in the future and that is why the Evil One stalks him so closely. It is a sure sign that Matthew is called to the Kingdom of God. We continue to pray for victory in this battle of the spirit and will not be downhearted. Please continue to pray for his healing and salvation, and those of his close friends, Nosher, Spike and Guido.

Christmas is a time to celebrate, but not to sleep. We will be tirelessly spreading Jesus' Love to the community even on Christmas Day itself. We know that many of the local shops and businesses will not be closing, even on Our Lord's Birthday. We must help them.

Pray for us, as we do God's work in a town sorely in need of guidance.

You will all be in our prayers.

Donald and Jeannie, Matthew and Mary

THE FRESH EXPAT

Eleanor Adams was fine in London. She juggled a part-time career in PR, a successful, handsome husband, David, and her two lovely children Chrystabel and Bettina.

But when they were moved to Hong Kong (David was made a partner in his property firm), she was out of her depth.

She finds herself overawed by the cliquey expatriate community. She misses her family and friends, and it would never occur to her to talk to the Chinese. She finds them 'too inscrutable'.

Even so, she sends a Round Robin to all her friends, to show them what a wonderful life she has. After all, she has everything her friends back home dream of, and she would hate them to see that it hasn't made her happy.

December 9

Dear All,

Sorry to write one of these general letters, but there's lots to tell, and it would take ages to write to you all! We're settled in our new home, a very smart, spacious apartment with views across to Repulse Bay. The floor-to-ceiling windows are a bit worrying and the view down is scary, but partners at Templetons always have the penthouse, and they're paying, so ours is not to reason why. Like the brochure says, "Templetons knows property"!

We've been here four months, so it's a good time to tell you a bit about life in HK. We have an Olympic-sized pool, four squash courts, a gym and a sauna, a beautician and even a diamond shop right in the compound. I hate to think what it would cost in London, and I'm very glad we're not paying for it.

But the biggest change in our lives is we have a maid, a Filipina called Gustaz. Eat your heart out Nigella, Gustaz is a *real* domestic goddess! She cooks, she cleans, she irons, she mops, she shops, she runs Bettina, Chrystabel and David from dawn to midnight. I never thought I'd want someone living in my home, dressing my children and cooking my family meals like this, but I'm getting used to it, through gritted teeth sometimes. Gustaz gets the girls up in the morning, cooks their breakfast, washes up and packs their schoolbags while David gets the car ready. I used to have a job, a family and a home to run. Now I have a maid.

The one flaw in this lovely apartment is that there isn't really a room for Gustaz, because David wanted it for his cross-trainer machine and his new Bose, so she makes herself comfy on the floor in Bettina and Chrystabel's room. I know, I know, but when you see how some people make their maids sleep in the kitchen, you realise how lucky Gustaz must think she is.

They say expats here work hard and play hard, and David definitely does, especially now he's a partner. It's Singapore one week, Beijing or

Bangkok another, weekends golfing in the New Territories or sailing off Phuket, all in the name of Templeton's corporate entertainment. The property market is very depressed at the moment, so he's working long hours.

I find I have a lot of time in the evenings, especially since Gustaz takes care of the girls. They've both fitted in to The British School – my girls in private school! I'm just glad that Templetons are footing the bill. Gustaz is always taking them off for weekends with new friends. It's the time I like to spend alone in the flat. My quiet time, I call it.

Expats here are a close-knit community, and it's sometimes a bit difficult. Some of the people at the British Club seem quite friendly, although actual conversation is taking longer than I wanted it to. The shopping is wonderful, too, especially at Stanley Market and on Tsim Tsa Shui, although it's funny seeing Chinese dressed up as Santa.

One strange thing is I've started getting lots of allergies. There must be something out here that doesn't agree with me. Sally, this woman at the Club, told me about this Dr Chow, who's a holistic healer who works with a lot of expats here. He's expensive, but he's amazing. He's got me on a new gluten-free, low-lactose diet, and it seems to be working. But migraines still keep me in bed some mornings, and I often feel a bit ache-y after lunch. Still, nothing a swift G&T doesn't cure. This is expat life, after all!

Now he's a partner, David's package gives us all Business Class flights home once a year, and we'll be staying at Mum and Dad's in Matlock in the last fortnight in July. It would be wonderful to see as many of you as possible, really.

All our love for a Happy Christmas, and Gong Xi Fa Cai as they say here (it means Happy New Year!)

Looking forward to the summer.

Lots of Love,

Eleanor, David, Bettina and Chrystabel

THE NORTH LONDON JEWISH MATRIARCH

Ruth Herzog wears a lot of black since her husband died early in the year.

Now 70, she sits at home on an antique Viennese chaise-longue waiting for her brilliant children to visit her.

Driven to over-achieve by Ruth's high expectations, they are a constant source of pride and disappointment to her. Sometimes one, sometimes the other, and she controls the family by never letting them know which one it will be.

She has lived all her life in North London, surrounded by intellectuals and respected artists, in the hope some of it would rub off on her children.

She sends her Round Robins to a diaspora of equally strong-willed, competitive Jewish matriarchs all over the world.

3 Archway Gardens
Hampstead
London

Dear All,

My first Christmas without Moshe will be quieter, but my children are here at my knee. Isaac my oldest, the lawyer, became the youngest non-Gentile to take Silk in a generation although how he works with those people I'll never know, criminals some of them, would steal your car as soon as look at you. But he married that nice girl he met on the kibbutz in Ma'alot Tarshiha, Rebecca I sometimes see reading the news on the BBC. They laid on a good Bar-Mitzvah for Simeon at Kenwood House, and his middle daughter Noam just eight and already she sings like Shirley Temple. Isaac also follows in my dear Moshe's footsteps as chairman at the British Textiles Commission, which would have made his Father so proud if he'd still been alive. "I do it for Pa," Isaac tells me which eases my pain at his loss. Such a good boy, Isaac.

Daughter Rachel the lecturer accepted the chair in Quantum Mechanics at Kings College just so she could stay close to her old Ma. A dutiful daughter is a blessing in old age. Her boys Mordechai and Levi still come to visit often and Mordechai, 12, studies hard and is top of his year once again at Haberdashers. His teachers say he's clever which I tell him will buy only so many matzohs, so I tell him he has to work hard to make something of himself like his grandfather did. Levi, who is 17, has won another music scholarship and will be touring Europe in March with The London Symphony Orchestra. You see, when I gave him his grandfather's violin all those years ago, I knew he wouldn't be a disappointment to me. They grow up so fast! I already have my eye on some nice girls for them.

But Binyamin our youngest, the surgeon so a Mister now not even a Doctor any more, continues to bring pain to his old mother's heart. Education I gave him, a good home I supplied, and now he marries out. "But Ma, Hao Ling and I are in love," he says, and how much good does love do me when Rabbi Shlomo calls? And her job if you can call it such a thing, what kind of job is editing Vogue for a respectable woman for all she is the mother of my son's children? And the grandchildren seem to wear what they like these days, although young Kylie is kind to her old grandmother.

But I'm learning, I'm studying, you have to keep in touch with the youth, so I'm doing psychoanalytical training at the Anna Freud Institute in Hampstead. I talk to Kylie about her dreams, travel with her on her night-time journeys and maybe bring her back home to me one day. And she's such a creative child, so talented, only seven and already Grade 8 on the cello and a Merit so soon in her LAMDA bronze medal. A bronze at age seven, they tell me is good enough. The other children seem to be have good points, too, with Jason getting a respectable 12 As in his GCEs, and Sophie the scholarship to Cambridge. I can still be proud of them, for all their father breaks my heart.

I hope you are well although how should I know? No one writes any more, no one even calls. This time of year, cards I used to get, now it's bills. It's a blessing I have children who at least know how to look after their old mother and make me proud.

I'm getting old. I still hold the family together, but I never know when it will turn round and strike me down or when it will come along and lift me high. The stories, I keep. The histories of the family I pass on to the grandchildren. And I know my Moshe is looking down and saying "Ruth, my girl, you're doing good, you're doing all right."

Write to me. Call. I'm always here.

Ruth.

THE KIWI SQUATTER

Jake Hoon is a sporting god. He's tall, well-built, athletic and handsome, with a rough-and-roguish charm the girls all fancy.

Not as much as he fancies himself, though.

He thinks women are only good for one thing. Two if you count cooking. OK, three if there's any cleaning to be done.

He's over from New Zealand for a year or so, 'bludging' a place to stay. But beware: offer him a place for a couple of nights till he's found his feet, and six weeks later those feet are still firmly under your table.

He sends his Round Robins to his mates back in New Zealand, to tell them exactly how much sex he's having. This letter does not go to his mother.

Dear All,

I don't like to brag, mates, but let me tell you, the girls here are hot! It's been girls, girls and more girls ever since I landed. You sit back and crack open a tinnie while I run down the list.

DENISE: shacked up with this little honey up near Wales. Remember that bloke from Pershore Cricket Club was in Auckland over December, said I was the kind of fast bowler they needed in the All-England Village League, which is like national level cricket, eh? He flew me over and I was set. Pommie batsmen are women! I tell you, it was like lamping wallabies with a .22!! Pershore's kind of out in the wop-wops, but I got a job in a pub where I pulled Denise. She's a real cracker, and does it all. Shacked up with her for a month but piked out when she went back to her husband who it turned out was only the bloody captain of the cricket team. I had to go bush for a bit and met **SANDRA**.

This bloke gave me a job at this kid's school near Oxford, teaching PE. Soft little beggars these Pommie kids, they just do what they're told. But Sports Day was hot and so were the mums, and I shacked up with this divorcee Sandy in her place in Oxford. Bit daggy having her kid in my class, but a real cracker for her age and the older chicks are always more grateful, know what I mean, eh? Drops her gear for a naughty any time. But she got heavy, so after a couple of months I nicked away to Birmingham where I met **PHILLIPPA & SUZANNE**.

That's right, mates, 2 of them! It's true what they say about nurses being dirty, if you get a good one. I tell you what, if you want to give the ferret a good run, you work in a pub over here. I'm not a bloke to boast, but the two things I heard most were "Four pints of lager, darling," and "what time do you get off, big boy?" They love the kiwi accent, too right? And I've got the best line. You look them in the eye and say "Lord of the Rings, eh? Yeah, I was an orc..." They love it. I pulled Pip + Su in this pub, and shacked up with them in their nurse's hostel. They said I could bludge on the floor, but it worked out better taking it in turns in their beds, eh? Turned out Pip's right on the snarky side, though, so I packed a wobbly and went bush smartish again to London, because that's where the action is, fair go? I'd only been there a week before I was cracking onto **ANTONIA.**

I tell you what, mates, the girls are a different class down London way. They like it a bit smoother so I had to change my line to "Lord of the Rings, eh? Yeah, I was an elf..." Toni was this posho two-pot screamer I met in a pub in Earls Court. Shacked up with her in her dad's flat in Kensington, and she took her trophy bloke round all these smart parties. I could tell none of the pommie blokes there were doing it for the girls, so you should get over here quick and get a piece of the action before I have it all! But it panned out Toni was a bit of a yacker, so I gave her the flick. Besides, by then I'd met **DONNA, KITTY, BAMBI + ILONA.** That's right, mates, 4 of them! And if they sound like porno stars, that's because they are! There's nothing they won't do once the cameras start rolling. This bloke in the pub said I had the looks for movies. I went in, cracked a fat for a screen test and left those pommie blokes for dead in the corner! They ran out of film before I'd finished! Now I'm in this crash hot place off the Tottenham Court Road shacked up with these 4 and let me tell you, we spend our nights rehearsing! The next flick, A Bow Job at Christmas, I have to unwrap them all. I play the christmas tree — I'm the wood, fair go?

I tell you what, mates, this is the place to be! There's space on the floor if you want to come over — and if there are any girls left after I've done them, they're all yours. cheers, Jake

THE DOTING NEW PARENTS

Alison and Graham Rankin had baby Harry in September, and think he is the most beautiful, talented and advanced baby in the world. Actually, Harry's quite normal.

Alison stopped being an estate agent to worship Harry full time. Graham still works as a marketing manager for a company that makes ice-cream.

They live in a smartened-up former council house in Isleworth, which smells faintly of stale milk and nappies.

Normally they send their Round Robins to close friends. This year it's going to everyone they've ever met.

Graham is trying to stop Alison breastfeeding, so he can get more involved by feeding Harry himself.

Alison only dimly remembers having a husband.

Harry, meanwhile, is thinking about bosoms.

From: yummy_harry@mothersmilk.com
Sent: 05:24 am
To: Simply everyone
Subject: Best Christmas Present EVER!

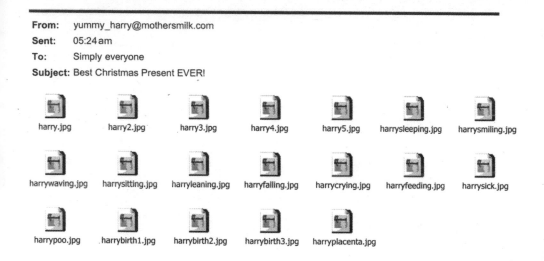

harry.jpg   harry2.jpg   harry3.jpg   harry4.jpg   harry5.jpg   harrysleeping.jpg   harrysmiling.jpg

harrywaving.jpg   harrysitting.jpg   harryleaning.jpg   harryfalling.jpg   harrycrying.jpg   harryfeeding.jpg   harrysick.jpg

harrypoo.jpg   harrybirth1.jpg   harrybirth2.jpg   harrybirth3.jpg   harryplacenta.jpg

Dear All,

How many ways do we love little Harry? Let us count the ways!

1 tiny little nose, as cute as a button.
2 big blue eyes, with long curly eyelashes his Mummy would die for.
3 o'clock in the morning, special snuggly time for Mummy.
4 chubby little limbs, as soft and sweet as marshmallow pies.
5 pudgy little fingers on each hand.
10 tiny toes, so small, so precious!
And 1,000,000 kisses on the most perfect tiny baby's perfect tiny cheeks!

Yes, Harry Jonathan Rankin was born on the 17th September at 4.13am, weighing in at a yummy 7lbs 13oz, after a 23-hour labour of love. Just days after he was born, we could tell there was something specially gorgeous about him, and we asked Dr Johnson (my gynae, who knows me inside out!) how to enroll Harry in a gifted kids programme. He seemed surprised, and told us that Harry is a normal, healthy baby. How wonderful to hear that from a doctor!

He's got a tiny tuft of the most gorgeous blond hair that sticks straight up (Harry, that is, not Dr Johnson!!). He's got the sweetest little pinkie-winkie. And he's got swirly-whirly tummy button, and a wurgly round tummy (we call him Harry

Posset!). And he's as bright as a button! Graham is sure he recognises him, and says "Daddy" when he gives him a cuddle. Dr Johnson seemed quite cross and said this was unlikely, but then he just doesn't spend as much time with Harry as we do.

He's got a terrific pair of lungs on him, and we're sure he could be a famous opera singer or rock star one day he's already so talented. He waves his arms and crosses them over his little chest and goes "Ooop! Ooop!", so maybe he'll be a rapper. They can be white these days, can't they? You should see the way he kicks, too! Even when he was in mummy's tum-tum, we thought he was going to play for Manchester United, and now we're sure. We asked Dr Johnson if there was a danger of him hurting himself, and he said "Look, Harry's fine. Babies just do that. All of them." So with so many following him like that, Harry looks like he'll be a real leader of men.

Sometimes, when he lies there at night sleeping, it's almost as if there's a golden aura of beauty around him. Since Dr Johnson doesn't really seem to "get" Harry, we've started taking him to a specialist, Dr Manley, who is a bit expensive and also didn't see the aura, but she explained to us that Harry is a perfectly normal baby. So lovely to hear a doctor call him perfect!

Must dash – we have to get the house ready for Harry's first Christmas. Graham's been shopping since November for the best educational toys to stimulate his tiny brain, and a series of baby-gyms to get him in trim. I've started a Montessori training to give him the best start we can, and I'm putting out a giant inflatable Santa with lights on the roof to introduce him to cultural icons. We're a family now, and we want Harry to really see how much that means.

Lots of love,

Alison, Graham and Harry

THE PREMATURE RETIREE

Angus and Deirdre Wilson had it all worked out.

A sensible savings plan, then at age 65 a well-planned dotage in France, surrounded by all their cronies for barbecues and bridge evenings.

Then, disaster struck. Angus was made redundant at 57. Too old to get another job, and too young to retire. He may have been an accountant, but the sums just didn't add up.

He couldn't afford France any more, so he had to look further afield.

A long way further afield.

Romania isn't quite what he'd planned, but he's putting on a brave face, and sending his Round Robin to his friends who are still employed, and still looking at Provence.

Chez Nous,
8 Ceausescu Strada,
Sprobanvetsia,
Cluj-Napoca,
Romania

Out with the Old, In with the New!

This is the life! While you poor lot were shivering in the rain over there, we've been enjoying a long hot summer like most Englishmen only dream about. Now I sit by the fire, glass of rude red in hand, looking out at a Bing Crosby–white Christmas draped across a landscape that's scarcely changed since the Middle Ages. None of your cluttering up the place with motorways and satellite towns! It's all as Nature intended. This is an amazing country! Rolling rural rides, ancient oak forests, undiscovered and untouched – we feel privileged to be in the vanguard of Brits discovering it. Believe us, in a few years, they'll be queuing up. The local villagers have welcomed us with open arms, and are forever popping round with a bucket of pickled cabbage, or even a leg of what we think was probably donkey. We didn't get that in Bicester, let me tell you!

Goodbye to all that!

To recap on an eventful year, the writing was on the wall in the tax department, and not to beat about the proverbial, at 57 if a chap's got his head screwed on straight he can see there's no sense banging his head against a barn door, even with my years of hard–earned experience. I could have spent another couple of years frittering away the nest–egg and having doors slammed in my face by inexperienced young executives who are still wet behind the ears. That's just one of the many things wrong with Britain these days. Instead we got smart, sold the house, cashed the whole lot in and skipped the country to warmer, greener and more affordable pastures new.

Je Ne Regrette Rien!

Of course, what with it all happening a few years ahead of schedule, and with the frankly insulting pay–out when you think of all I did for that company, we had to rethink our taste of Toujours Provence, and cut our chateau according to our cloth. A redundancy cheque stretches much more the further you go from the

South-East, and now a restful retirement beckons in Sprobanvetsia, a village just outside the bustling metropolis of Cluj-Napoca, just three hours from Bucharest. Talk about perfect timing! We caught this place just before the property boom that's bound to happen, and snapped up a splendid stone-built country residence for the price of semi in Banbury, and enough in the bank to tide us over the next few years, if we're prudent.

Remember, You Heard It Here First!

Romania's the kind of place a chap can settle. For the life of me, I can't imagine why people haven't been flocking here. This place is going to skyrocket, and then we'll be sitting on a nice little investment! I grant you it's had a rocky past, but you could say the same for anywhere in Europe. Even La Belle France was a bit of a no-go zone for a while, if you think about it. Turn your nose up at anywhere with a lively history and you end up in Switzerland, and I can assure you property prices there are no laughing matter.

Keep The Home Fires Burning!

Besides, after all our summer holidays house hunting in Provence, Romania's a doddle. There's an old market every Thursday, just like the one we used to shop at in Avignon, except there are rather more root vegetables, and we have to take our chickens home live and pluck them ourselves, which came as a bit of a surprise to Deirdre. But what odds, when a bottle of entirely drinkable vin rouge comes in at less than 30p? At prices like that it's easy enough to tuck away a bottle or two over lunch without it breaking the bank. The nightly power-cuts add a dash of charm, and the old place is all the more bewitching by candlelight, if chilly. Sometimes, when there's a full moon, we see the villagers surrounding the house with burning torches, which is welcoming. In the morning, we find our tyres have been let down, which we assume is their way of saying they don't want us to leave. Delightful people!

Now, if we can share our good fortune and tempt any of you fine folk to join us for a week or two, drop us a line. The phones are down at the mo, but the mail seems to get through!

Happy Christmas,

Angus and Deirdre

Angus and Deirdre

THE GAP-YEAR SCHOOLBOY

Felix DeMoubrey left Repton with better A-levels than anyone expected, so his parents are paying for him to have a gap year in Asia and Australia, before he goes to study Anthropology at Edinburgh.

He keeps in touch with his school friends via e-mail, which he accesses in Internet cafés. He's taken some ace photos on his new Canon digi-max, which cost him a month's wages working for the old man's law firm over the summer. He has plans to put them on his website, but never gets round to it.

While the temples are interesting and the food is exotic, what Felix really wants is to hitch up with some hot Ozzie girls.

He may have left England as an eighteen-year-old schoolboy, but he's determined to return home a Man.

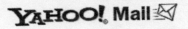

Subject: Christmas Massage from Bangkok

Date: Wed, 11 12:34:30 +0100

From: "Felix" <chilled_dude23@freenet.com.uk>

To: ludo47@yahoo.co.uk

Dear All,

Hi gentlemen – that actually means you Jess, Ludo, Tommo, Monster, Chewie, Shifty and all the other Repton Rebels. Oh, and hello Mum, hello Dad. I've made it to Bangkok, and it's cool here – yeah, yeah, I know it's hot actually.

Really amazing thing happened in Vientiane (capital of Laos, not Vietnam, how confusing is that?). I was staying in a seriously cheap backpacker place (only 4,000 dong a night, which is even cheaper than Chewie at the end of term – oops, sorry mate!!!) and it turns out the other guy in the dorm was the guy from Sherborne who broke Ludo's arm in the Sevens last winter. Amazing, really small world. Says he remembers you, too, Shifty. Ooo-er! Anything we should know about?

A lot's happened in the last five months, some of it I can tell you here, some of it's for your ears only back home. Are we still meeting in May at Via's stepmum's place in Umbria? I'll have a tan to show off and some stories to tell, believe me!

India was cool, saw the Taj Mahal the Red Fort and the Palace of the Winds (much curry, my friends!) at Jaipur or Jodhpur or Jampot or something like. Bit of a haze actually thanks to some truly amazing… ah that wood be telling, wooden tit, if you know what I mean – and I know you do! Had Delhi belhi (which was velhi velhi bad!!!!) from this seriously cheap backpacker place in Trivandrum. This guy in a taxi gave me some brown powder he said would help – gentlemen, I haven't seen stars like that since the Christmas Snakebite boat race. (Oops, sorry Mum, never told you about that!)

Another amazing thing happened in Mumbai (that's Bombay to you, Dad). Ran into a bunch of guys from Ampleforth, and they really were the wild boys of Wonga. Remember the Demon Cow Topplers we heard about from Habs second XI in the summer? It was them!!!! Let's hope the long arm of Officer Plod doesn't read this letter! Anyways, stayed in a seriously cheap backpacker place, (only 500 rupees a night that's the price of a pint) which was cool except for that Ghandi bloke having his revenge again (I think I must be as thin as him by now!).

Ran into Tash and Harvey in Malacca, and they were – wait for it – bashing Old Man Beaufort's plastic and staying in the Hyatt! It's not exactly authentic travel, is it? Used their shower, grabbed some stuff out of their minibar and headed out to a seriously cheap backpacker place a couple of miles out of town near an industrial estate. And, mios amigos, it doesn't get more real than that!

Met a couple of Ozzie gents on their way to England and gave them Tommo's address in case they need somewhere to stay for a night. No worries with that, eh mate? They can always go in the West Wing, eh, old boy?

Had to do family duty in Singapore with Uncle Ted (Lord of the Bored) and Auntie ("Call Me Jules") Julia. Boooooring!!!! All they wanted to talk about was life back in England and ask me how school was. Honestly! It's like I haven't actually just gone halfway round the world!

Moved on swift-ish, and I'm in Bangkok (tho I haven't done that yet – are they girls? are they boys? I dunno! I dunno! And little details like that matter to some of us, Monster!). Staying in this little backpacker place, seriously cheap, but gotta go now, guy next door keeps hammering on the wall and saying something about a beach…(!)

Have a good Crimbo, gentlemen, and see you in La Bella Italia in May. Take it easy… but take it!!!! (oops, sorry Mum!)

Namaste, Sawadee, Ciao, whatever –

Felix

THE LIFE ENHANCEMENT COACH

Annette Wilkins believes in herself.

She also believes she can help other people find their true direction in life.

Now 40, after twelve years in human resources, she has trained as a Life Enhancement Coach. Her life is a holistic hash of New Age mumbo-jumbo and Management College consultant-speak. And walking on hot coals.

Her outlook on life is overwhelmingly positive, and she likes to know best.

Annette is also business savvy and wants to make money.

She runs her business, Reach for the Skies! Ltd, from her three-bedroom semi in Pinner.

Her Round Robins hope to convert all her sceptical friends, and to show how enhanced and rewarding her life is.

"If you believe in yourself, great things will happen –
Go Reach For The Skies!"

Take control and feel the change! A New Year means a New You! When someone moves your cheese, chase it – and bring the pickle! When I look at all the changes I have made in my life over the past year, I see it as a remarkable, holistic, personal journey of self–fulfillment, self–empowerment and self–control. I cannot lead if you will not follow – so walk with me!

Reach For The Skies has really taken off. Several human resources departments in the locality have embraced the changes that I can bring to their companies. Both Siffenham Nuclear Power Station and the Virology Research Board at Bigglesbury had been experiencing high levels of staff churn and absenteeism due to ill health. My interventions have made a great impact on staff morale and levels of individual empowerment. They found my visualisation techniques involving hot sun and cellular recomposition very liberating, and we were able to facilitate self–management changes that improved their performance projectionability and reactualised their commitment levels.

I was also most fortunate to meet Vivien Seeker, an inspiring journalist from *ME!* magazine, at the *Visualisation and Fire Walking* conference in Manchester, and she wrote a great article on me, which has raised Reach for the Skies' profile. Vivien wasn't deterred by the large blisters she sustained on her feet, after I had assured her that it sometimes takes time to cross the boundaries to control your physical reactions. She filed her story from the Burns Unit in Eastwickbury Hospital, which is a testament to the new commitment and direction she has found in her life.

Personally, I have delved deep within myself to retain my desired weight with a new diet and exercise regime I learnt from the great Indian yogi, Guru Gunarajan, in his inspirational book *Yogi, Yoghurt, Yoga and You.* As a result I am now seeing Bernard, a gorgeous feng shui expert from Cardiff, who I met at the *Whose Destiny Is It Anyway?* conference in Brighton last year. For a long time I'd had worries that things were not totally in harmony at home, so I had a good excuse to ask him over. After painting my front door red, then green, then red again and re-hanging it four times, we had made a real connection on a very deep level. I supported him at the *Healing Houses* conference in Leatherhead in the spring, where he spoke on the holistic realignment of home furnishing for enhancing human relationships. It has been a wonderful summer and finding my soul mate has all been down to my work last year on visualising your perfect partner, as in Jill Davies' holistically inspiring book *Can I Love You Like I Love Me?*

A wise man once told me this story, which I'd like to share with you. Two frogs fell into a bucket of milk. One gave up, and drowned. But one was determined to stay afloat. All night he kicked and swam, until in the morning, the farmer opened his milk churn to find – it was full of butter, and the frog, still alive, was sitting on the top! Now, this farmer was French, and seeing a frog with such meaty legs already pre-buttered, he ate it. When he found the second frog, and ate that one too, but was disappointed with its skinny legs. An inspirational story, and one in which anyone will find their own personal message. Ask yourself – what kind of legs do I have?

I hope your year ends with you on top of the butter, and Season's Greetings to you all. Remember YOU are the controller of your destiny! May the New Year bring forth all you dream of, and may you become the person that you aspire to be.
Yours as ever,

Annette
Annette

THE REMARKABLY DULL FAMILY

Mandy and Colin Gray are the people who people forgot.

Mandy is a part-time nurse, while Colin is in middle-management. They have two children.

They live in a medium-sized house on a new-ish estate, convenient for the schools, the High Street and the railway station.

They grew up in the same town, met at the same school and held hands behind the bike shed at the same railway station.

The highlight of their year is when Dulux adds another tone of pale brown to their soft sheen non-drip emulsion range.

Someone exactly like them lives four doors down from you, and they all send Round Robins to each other.

They are quietly happy.

12, Crochet Close, Shrewsbury, Shropshire

Dear All

We've had a nice year. It's funny how the year flies by it's so busy, but when you come down to write about it, it's hard to know what to say.

The house is looking nice. This year we repainted the lounge in parchment, which is a nice change from the old magnolia. We put some decking from Homebase at the end of the garden, just like Alan Titchmarsh. It looks very nice. Sometimes in the summer we had our tea out there. The trains going by didn't disturb us too much.

John is 15, and growing into a nice young man. His voice has broken and he has a good nose on him. We bought him some special cream for his spots and they look much better. He still loves his football and has been teaching Robert a few tactics. Saturdays often find us down at the park watching them play. They are such nice boys to have around the house and a typical evening conversation goes like this:

John – "What's for tea, Mum?"
Me – "Chicken nuggets, chips and beans."
Robert – "Great."
John – "Yeah."

Then they go off and play computer games in their rooms until I call them down.

Robert is now 13, likes school and is learning the electric guitar. His Nan gave him one for his birthday, which is quite loud. He has a girlfriend, Sally, but he doesn't talk about her. Both boys are doing well in school, and like their teachers. Robert is especially good at Geography, and came ninth in his class. They have some nice friends who come round to the house sometimes after school to play computer games. Robert says he'd like to be a policeman when he grows up, and John wants to run a sports shop.

Colin is still manager at Boots. He continues to enjoy his bowling and he has been doing up the caravan for next year's holiday in the Lake District. He has put a new TV in, in case of bad weather. We had a nice fortnight up there this summer in a little site near Ambleside, although it was a shame that this year it rained a little bit more than usual. The boys liked the arcades though and for me it was nice to not have to cook, because there are so many little cafes and Colin and the boys like their fish and chips.

My Dad had a funny little turn in the autumn so I've been helping Mum out at home, as well as doing a few days' supply nursing at the old folks home. But mostly I'm kept out of trouble just cleaning the house, and taking Robert and John to and from school. I enjoy my big shop at Tesco's where there are always so many bargains to be found. We have been collecting their points and I hope to have enough for a foot spa soon, although Colin says he'd like a new wheelbarrow.

Hope you are all well and have had a nice year too.
Happy Christmas
Love,

Mandy, Colin, John and Robert

THE DIVINE BEING

God is a deity. He lives in Heaven, and everywhere else at the same time.

He likes to travel and meet people.

He is divine, which is nice, but has moments of self-doubt when He worries that He might have made a bit of a bish of some things.

He is all-seeing, all-powerful and in all places at all times.

He's the first to admit that He doesn't know everything, though. But being immortal, He reassures Himself that there is still plenty of time.

Cloud 7,
Heaven

Dear All,

Well, another mixed year, some of it good (my fault) and
some of it bad (not). Rather more war than I'd planned. Sorry.
I suppose on hindsight I should have thought the oil through
a bit more carefully. At the time it seemed quite a good
thing to do with those prehistoric rainforests. Mind you,
if I'd known then that you were going to chop down so many
of the new ones, I'd have kept the old ones going a few
millennia longer. Less oil, more trees, two birds with one
stone (and I know I'm inclined to cast the first of those).

Otherwise, I've been very busy, which is all part and
parcel of being omnipotent. When you <u>can</u> do everything, you
end up feeling you <u>should</u> do everything. I've also travelled
a lot. Everywhere actually. Something to do with being in
all places at all times. It has its drawbacks, of course.
You know that old advert, "Getting There is Half The Fun"?
Well, that's the half I never get, because wherever it is,
I'm always and already there. Still, mustn't grumble. It's
an imperfect world , after all, I read somewhere. Think it
was The Spectator.

Must go now. Have to buy something for The Boy. Always a
tricky fellow to shop for. What do you give the man who has
nothing? Although I don't know why I bother. Whatever I
give him he giveth unto the poor, usually before Boxing Day.

Still, have a good festive season, and keep up the sing-
ing. I love it. Really love it. Especially that one with
the reindeers. You can miss out a few of those hosannas and
alleluias, and bump up the reindeers if you like. What's his
name - Randolph? Love him.

Anyway, Happy Christmas to you All. Oh, sorry. I mean
Happy Holidays, of course. Still can't get used to that.

All my love (and that's a lot!) and best wishes for next year,

God

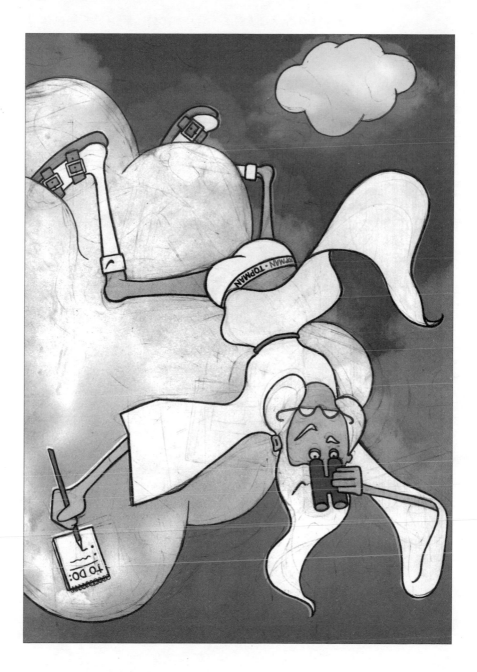

BEYOND COINCIDENCE

Martin Plimmer and Brian King

Laura Buxton, aged ten, releases a balloon from her garden in Staffordshire. It lands 140 miles away in Wiltshire, in the garden of another Laura Buxton, aged ten. Two sisters in Alabama decide, independently, to visit each other. En route, their identical jeeps collide and both are killed. Coincidence? Or something beyond coincidence?

Sceptics see only the laws of probability at work. But what are the odds against mathematician Ian Stewart being struck by a meteorite moments after discussing the odds of such a thing happening?

Beyond Coincidence is a celebration of the Universe's most beguiling phenomenon, containing more than 200 amazing stories of coincidence and many intriguing insights into its workings. Next time you bump into your bank manager in the Amazonian rainforest, you may understand why...

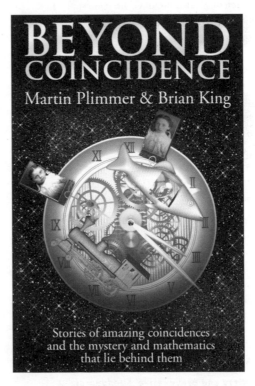

'**Amazing**' Simon Hoggart, *Guardian*

'**A first-rate book**' *Observer*

'**Entertaining and intelligent**'
Mail on Sunday

'**Guaranteed to send a shiver down your spine**' *Good Book Guide*

UK £12.99   ISBN 1 84046 534 4

(available in paperback from January 2005, UK £6.99, ISBN 1 84046 618 9)

OTHER TITLES AVAILABLE FROM ICON BOOKS

BETWEEN YOU AND I: A LITTLE BOOK OF BAD ENGLISH
James Cochrane • Introduced by John Humphrys

Here is a new, enlarged edition of the book described by *The Independent* as a 'cool, disdainfully precise A–Z of linguistic misuse', and by its author as 'a two-hour course in language detoxification'. Included as an appendix for the first time is George Orwell's 1946 essay 'Politics and the English Language'.

Much of what is included here is 'half-educated' language used by people in the mistaken belief that speaking or writing in their natural idiom is somehow less 'correct'. Most of the examples come from people who should know better: from public figures, from those in the media and politics, from teachers and university academics. It is a sad paradox that while our language is constantly being enriched from below it is all too often being impoverished from above.

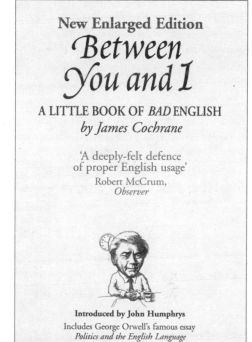

New Enlarged Edition
Between You and I
A LITTLE BOOK OF *BAD* ENGLISH
by James Cochrane

'A deeply-felt defence of proper English usage'
Robert McCrum,
Observer

Introduced by John Humphrys
Includes George Orwell's famous essay
Politics and the English Language

Fortunately, although the situation has probably deteriorated since the first edition, it's not too late for the worst examples of Bad English to be recognised and remedied. Many readers may be surprised to find that much of what they thought was 'bad' English is in fact perfectly good, and that what they have been led to think of as 'good' English is sometimes ignorant, dishonest or plain stupid.

'**A deeply-felt defence of proper English usage**' Robert McCrum, *Observer*

'**Witty and provocative**' *Sunday Herald*

'**A cool, disdainfully precise A–Z of linguistic misuse**' Terence Blacker, *Independent*

UK £9.99   ISBN 1 84046 605 7

THE UNFAIR SEX

Nina Farewell Illustrated by Roy Doty

All is fair in love and war, and for Nina Farewell the two are more similar than you might think. Ladies, come out on top in the battle of the sexes: learn how to get all that *you* want without giving men the one thing that *they* want.

Originally published in the 1950s, this timeless guide reveals the arsenal of devices, techniques and approaches a man deploys to get what he wants, and details the countermeasures a woman can take to come out on top.

LEARN...

The rewards of refusing – how to say No in every conceivable situation.

How to avoid, at all costs, going to a man's apartment... and what to do once you get there.

How to get what you want without giving him the one thing he wants.

UK £9.99   ISBN 1 84046 603 0

UK £20.00   ISBN 1 84046 606 5

OTHER TITLES AVAILABLE FROM ICON BOOKS

365: YOUR DATE WITH HISTORY
W.B. Marsh and Bruce Carrick

Every day of the year has a story to tell. Who was assassinated, acceded to the throne, fled from their country? Who was born, began an affair, was impeached, disgraced or knighted? What nation was born, what army defeated in the face of great odds?

365: Your Date with History is a fantastically browsable historical encyclopaedia, mapping the highs and lows of human existence throughout the year. W.B. Marsh and Bruce Carrick have often deliberately picked stories to surprise – the day Rommel, the Desert Fox, committed suicide; the Duchess of Richmond's ball three days before the Battle of Waterloo, Nelson joining the Navy at the age of twelve, and many more. Each day is packed with historical facts and sometimes brief, often more lengthy, stories from a dizzying array of subjects.

Wander back and forth through history day-by-day with 365 and become engrossed in this lovingly constructed wealth of historical anecdotes, written accessibly and with plenty of quirky humour. It will be a favourite to have around the house for years.